CAMBRIDGE LIBRARY COLLECTION

Books of enduring scholarly value

Cambridge

The city of Cambridge received its royal charter in 1201, having already been home to Britons, Romans and Anglo-Saxons for many centuries. Cambridge University was founded soon afterwards and celebrated its octocentenary in 2009. This series explores the history and influence of Cambridge as a centre of science, learning, and discovery, its contributions to national and global politics and culture, and its inevitable controversies and scandals.

Hobson's Conduit

It is a peculiarity of Cambridge that in one of the principal streets, Trumpington Street, there is a runnel of fresh water, called Hobson's Conduit, on either side of the road (a similar stream in St Andrew's Street was covered over in the 1990s). These streams form part of a system of water supply named after Thomas Hobson (1545–1631), the Cambridge carrier, from whom we get the expression 'Hobson's Choice', and for whom the young John Milton wrote two verse epitaphs, reproduced in this work. For 250 years, Hobson's Conduit provided the principal supply of drinking water for the centre of the city, after Andrew Perne (1519–89), Vice-Chancellor of the University, persuaded a number of patrons, including Hobson, to subscribe towards the project. First published in 1938, this history of Cambridge's ancient urban watercourse was written by W. D. Bushell, one of the trustees of the Hobson's Conduit Trust.

Cambridge University Press has long been a pioneer in the reissuing of out-of-print titles from its own backlist, producing digital reprints of books that are still sought after by scholars and students but could not be reprinted economically using traditional technology. The Cambridge Library Collection extends this activity to a wider range of books which are still of importance to researchers and professionals, either for the source material they contain, or as landmarks in the history of their academic discipline.

Drawing from the world-renowned collections in the Cambridge University Library, and guided by the advice of experts in each subject area, Cambridge University Press is using state-of-the-art scanning machines in its own Printing House to capture the content of each book selected for inclusion. The files are processed to give a consistently clear, crisp image, and the books finished to the high quality standard for which the Press is recognised around the world. The latest print-on-demand technology ensures that the books will remain available indefinitely, and that orders for single or multiple copies can quickly be supplied.

The Cambridge Library Collection brings back to life books of enduring scholarly value (including out-of-copyright works originally issued by other publishers) across a wide range of disciplines in the humanities and social sciences and in science and technology.

Hobson's Conduit

*The New River at Cambridge
Commonly Called Hobson's River*

W. D. BUSHELL

CAMBRIDGE
UNIVERSITY PRESS

CAMBRIDGE UNIVERSITY PRESS

Cambridge, New York, Melbourne, Madrid, Cape Town,
Singapore, São Paolo, Delhi, Tokyo, Mexico City

Published in the United States of America by Cambridge University Press, New York

www.cambridge.org
Information on this title: www.cambridge.org/9781108042444

© in this compilation Cambridge University Press 2012

This edition first published 1938
This digitally printed version 2012

ISBN 978-1-108-04244-4 Paperback

HOBSON'S CONDUIT

LONDON
Cambridge University Press
BENTLEY HOUSE, N.W. I

NEW YORK · TORONTO
BOMBAY · CALCUTTA · MADRAS
Macmillan

TOKYO
Maruzen Company Ltd

PLATE I

THOMAS HOBSON

HOBSON'S CONDUIT:

THE NEW RIVER AT

CAMBRIDGE

COMMONLY CALLED

Hobſon's River

By W. D. BUSHELL, *M.A.*, *Barriſter-at-Law*, and one of the *Truſtees* of HOBSON'S CONDUIT TRUST

With a *Preface* by E. JACKSON, *Esq.*, *Chairman* of the *Truſtees*, and *Ex-Mayor* of CAMBRIDGE, & J. A. VENN, *Esq.*, *Litt.D.*, *F.S.A.*, one of the *Truſtees*, & *Ex-Preſident* of the Cambridge Antiquarian Society

CAMBRIDGE
AT THE *Univerſity Preſs*
MCMXXXVIII

PREFACE

The expression "Hobson's choice" has long been a household word wherever the English language is spoken, but not many, even of Cambridge inhabitants, know anything about the man himself, and still fewer are familiar with the subsequent history of his public-spirited action in fostering that picturesque supply of water which, in its ultimate "runs", is so familiar a feature of our streets. A stroll along "Senior Wrangler's Walk" has all too frequently set topographical limits to the knowledge possessed by resident and stranger alike, whilst in regard to chronology the Lensfield Road monument has perforce sufficed to answer the more persistent of overseas visitors.

Now, however, matters have been rectified and, as representative Borough and University members of Hobson's Conduit Trust, we congratulate most warmly our fellow-member upon this admirable chronicle, wherein he traces, from "Nine Wells" to those obscure dipping-holes in the centre of the town, the course of the Cambridge New River, and describes the legal and other vicissitudes through which it has passed during the last three centuries. After fishing in it as boys, sailing model boats, and even skating upon its surface, one of us dwelt subsequently beside it for two decades as a riparian householder; the other has for many years been Chairman of its Trust. We are confident that, after the publication of this little volume, the affection we possess for our charge will be shared by a far wider circle, and its author thereby recompensed in the manner most gratifying to himself.

EDWARD JACKSON
17 Market Hill

J. A. VENN
The Lodge, Queens' College
Cambridge

AUTHOR'S NOTE

This history has been written for the use of the Trustees, but the number of people who are interested in the antiquities of Cambridge is so considerable that it has been thought worth while to publish it.

The document printed as Appendix III, to the existence of which in the Record Office Dr W. M. Palmer, F.S.A., kindly drew my attention, has not seen the light since it was written in 1575. The Order of a local Court of Sewers, dated 1634, and printed as Appendix IV, and the second and anonymous epitaph printed in Appendix I, are not readily accessible elsewhere. But beyond this the book does not claim to be a work of any great original antiquarian research; it is a compilation from sources, most of which, though inconveniently scattered, have long been available.

Several neighbours, particularly Mr J. H. Bullock, M.A., and Dr L. Cobbett, M.D., F.R.C.S., have shown their affection for the memory of Thomas Hobson by reading parts of my manuscript, making suggestions for its improvement, and by helping me in other ways, and to all of these I tender my thanks.

W. D. BUSHELL

March 1938

CONTENTS

Appendices

PLATES

MAPS

SOURCES

Of the numerous books and papers which have been consulted the following are the more important:

COOPER. *Annals of Cambridge.* By C. H. Cooper, 1842 and onwards.

CHARITY COMMISSION. Reports of the former Commissioners for Inquiring concerning Charities, Hobson's Conduit, vol. XXXI, 1837.

C.A.S. Cambridge Antiquarian Society. Proceedings and Publications. Various Articles.

WILLIS and CLARK. *The Architectural History of the University of Cambridge.* By R. Willis and J. W. Clark, 1886.

Papers in the hands of the Clerk to the Trustees.

Papers collected by the late Mr G. A. Matthew now in the Borough Library.

HOBSON'S CONDUIT

The New River AT CAMBRIDGE

CHAPTER I

THE OPEN WATERCOURSES IN THE STREETS OF CAMBRIDGE

It is a peculiarity of the town of Cambridge that in two of the principal streets, Trumpington Street and St Andrew's Street, there are runnels of fresh water flowing in open channels between the roadway and the footway on either side. These form part of a system of water supply, inaugurated in 1610, and commonly called Hobson's Conduit, after Thomas Hobson, the Cambridge carrier. This system, for two hundred and fifty years, provided the principal supply of drinking water for the centre of the town. As St Andrew's Street is narrow and apt to be encumbered with traffic, it has been found necessary in recent years to reduce the runnels in this street to very slight dimensions, but happily the pair in Trumpington Street still retain more of the form and of the volume of water of earlier days. These runnels of water in the streets are pleasant in appearance. In the history of sanitation they recall the days when an open watercourse down a street was the latest word in street cleansing, and in the history of Cambridge they recall the name of a distinguished citizen.

Another of the charms of Cambridge is the umbrageous entrance into the town by the London and Trumpington Road, and the character of this road depends on Hobson's River which here flows pleasantly under the trees of the Botanic Garden and through the lawns in front of Brookside.

Before entering upon the history of this water system, it may be well to point out that the word "conduit" is used to convey two rather different meanings. In view of its derivation it might be expected to denote merely the channel or pipe along which the water was made to flow, but long before the days of Thomas Hobson the word had come to denote also the fountain or other structure from which the water on its arrival in the town was distributed to the consumers. Thus, to some people, the words "Hobson's Conduit" would mean only the Jacobean structure, the old fountain, which now stands at the corner of Lensfield Road, but on the other hand the trust with which we are now concerned is officially designated "Hobson's Conduit Trust", under which designation it cares, not only for the old fountain, but also for the whole system of watercourses and pipes from the springs downwards.

A stranger reading this book may be puzzled by the names, Market Hill, Senate House Hill, Peas Hill, and so on, applied to sites in the town where there are no appreciable hills. In Cambridge only the Castle Hill is a hill in the usual sense of the word; elsewhere a hill means an open space amongst the houses such as would be called, in other towns, a place or a square. Similarly Norwich has its local word "plain", and speaks of Bank Plain, St Andrew's Plain, and so on. Open spaces in the town covered with grass are in some cases called Commons, but more often they are designated Fens, and not infrequently the word Piece, which is peculiar to Cambridge, is used.

St Andrew's Hill, which is often mentioned in these pages, was formerly a secondary market place for the town; it is called the fareyard in Lyne's map of 1574, the hogg market in Loggan's map of 1688, and the beast market in Custance's map of 1798. But it is now scarcely recognizable as a Cambridge hill or open space, because, as far back as 1842, the Town Council covered most of its area with a building which was used for thirty years as a Corn Exchange, but is now let by them to a private firm and used as a garage.

Spittle End, or Spittlehouse End, is the name formerly attached to the south end of Trumpington Street, at the point where Trumpington Street, Trumpington Road, Lensfield Road, and the Fen Causeway, now meet. It may now be called Lensfield Corner. The word Spittle does not refer to Addenbrooke's Hospital, for that institution is relatively modern—the founder out of whose bequest it was built did not die till 1719. The word refers to the old almshouses of St Anthony and St Eligius which stood on, and in front of, the sites of Nos. 6 and 7 Trumpington Street. The street is now a wide one at this point, but the almshouses were so far advanced

1-2

into it as to make it very narrow. The almshouses were pulled down in 1852 and rebuilt close by in Panton Street.

The old Botanic Garden too is often mentioned here. This is an area in the town bounded by Free School Lane, Pembroke Street, Corn Exchange Street and Peas Hill, which is now chiefly covered with museums and laboratories. In the eighteenth century there were buildings round the margin of this area, including the Perse Grammar School and the Perse Almshouses, while the inner part of it constituted the Botanic Garden. This garden, founded in 1760, continued on this site for some seventy years, after which the now existing Botanic Garden was created on the much larger site which adjoins the eastern bank of Hobson's River where it flows beside the Trumpington Road.

In Cambridge, as in other towns, various streets have changed their names in the course of the last three hundred years. The line of street which is now called, first Hobson Street and then King Street, was formerly called Walls Lane along the whole of its length; until the foundation of the Perse Grammar School the lane which is now called Free School Lane was known as Lutburne Lane; Guildhall Place was formerly Sparrow's Lane; Corn Exchange Street was Slaughterhouse Lane, and so on. In the following pages the modern name is generally used.

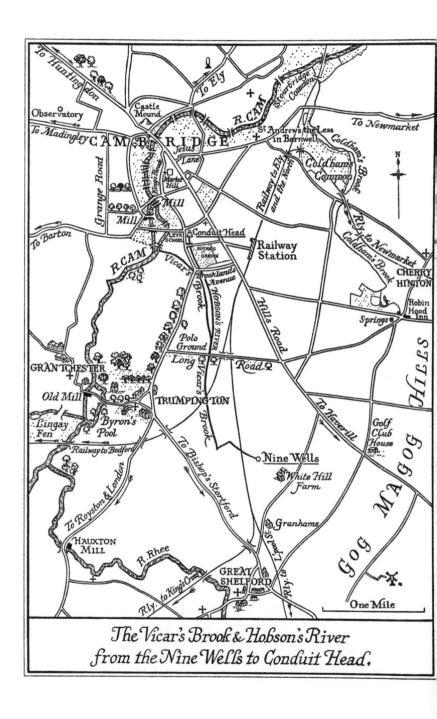

The Vicar's Brook & Hobson's River
from the Nine Wells to Conduit Head.

CHAPTER II

THE NINE WELLS, AND THE WATERCOURSE DOWN TO THE CONDUIT HEAD

Above Cambridge the first stream to flow into the Cam is the Vicar's Brook. The main road from Cambridge to Trumpington and London now crosses this brook by a brick culvert just south of the modern Brooklands Avenue. This brick culvert is known as Stonebridge, a name which may be a contraction of Milestone Bridge, as there stands upon it the first of the sixteen milestones which were set up between Cambridge and Barkway on the road to Ware and London soon after 1724 when the road was constituted a turnpike road. Until 1912 the Vicar's Brook was at this point the boundary between the borough of Cambridge and the rural parish of Trumpington, and it is still the boundary between ecclesiastical parishes. This crossing of the Vicar's Brook by the London Road was known for many generations as Trumpington Ford, although as far back as 1552 there was some sort of a bridge here,[1] perhaps only a footbridge. From here the Vicar's Brook flows down the boundary of Coe Fen into that part of the Cam which is the mill stream of the ancient King's Mill, falling into the river at the garden of the late Mr Hodgson opposite the municipal bathing-place for women. There is the less water passing under the Stonebridge because much of it has been abstracted by the artificial

[1] Cooper, vol. II, p. 47 note.

channel of Hobson's River, which takes off from the brook about half a mile above.

In and near the town of Cambridge the ground is composed of gravels and clays. But most of the south-east of the county of Cambridgeshire, including Newmarket and the Royston neighbourhood, is on the chalk upland which extends across England from Dorsetshire to Norfolk. This is the line of high ground along which runs the ancient Icknield Way. The well-marked north-western edge of this upland approaches to within three miles of the centre of the town of Cambridge. The high ground is here known as the Gog Magog Hills, recalling a figure, long since vanished, of a giant which, like the famous White Horse of Berkshire, was cut out on the hill-side,[1] a hillside which was then turfed though now under the plough: this figure was at Wandlebury Camp near the Linton Road. The north-western slope of this upland, facing the town of Cambridge, discloses the chalk marl, the geological bed at the bottom of the chalk. The chalk marl is impermeable, whereas the chalk above it is permeable to water, so that springs of water issue from the foot of the slopes at various points. There is one excellent spring near the Robin Hood Inn at Cherry Hinton. This gives rise to the Coldham Common stream. It is as near to the centre of Cambridge and is as copious as the springs which give rise to the Vicar's Brook, but the Coldham Common stream enters the Cam below Cambridge and below the weir at Jesus Lock, so that the engi-

[1] *William Cole of Milton*, by W. M. Palmer, p. 71.

neers of Hobson's day, having no steam power and relying entirely on gravitation, could not make much use of it. It is with another similar group of springs known as the Nine Wells that we are here concerned. These form the source of the Vicar's Brook. They are situated in a three-acre close in the parish of Great Shelford. In a plan in the possession of the Trustees the exact number of the springs, nine, are indicated, but most people will agree that the springs merge together and cannot be counted separately with any precision. The name, Nine Wells, is in fact a generic name in the south of Cambridgeshire; there are other groups of springs bearing the same name, notably a group between the villages of Whittlesford and Thriplow. The Nine Wells, the source of the Vicar's Brook, are close to the main line of railway which runs southward from Cambridge towards London, and the spot is marked by an obelisk which is easily visible to railway travellers.

The obelisk has four faces. The inscription which is turned northwards is as follows:

This supply of water to Cambridge from the adjacent springs was first suggested in 1574 by Andrew Perne Master of Peterhouse. The design was revived by James Montagu Master of Sidney Sussex, and in 1610 carried into effect at the joint expence of the University and Town.

The inscription which is turned eastwards reads:

Benefactors to the Watercourse and Conduit, Thomas Chaplin Esqre Lord of the Manor of Trumpington Dela-pole 1610, Stephen Perse M.D. Fellow of Gonville and Caius

1615, Thomas Hobson Carrier Cambridge and London 1630, Samuel Potts Alderman of Cambridge 1632, Joseph Merrill Alderman of Cambridge 1806.

The south face is blank, but on the west face it is recorded of the obelisk itself that it was "Erected by public subscription 1861, Charles Finch, Treasurer".

The name of the benefactor who died in 1632 is wrongly given, it was Edward Potto.[1] The treasurer of the subscription fund, Charles Finch, had been Mayor in 1848; he was the last of a family who, since 1688, had conducted on Market Hill the ironfounder's business which is still continued by Messrs Macintosh. The name Finch can still be read on the cast-iron railings of the causeway which leads to Garret Hostel Bridge. This Charles Finch was buried in Great Eversden churchyard, where his tombstone is still to be seen. As Hobson's water was of daily importance to those who lived on Market Hill, it is not surprising to find that several of this family were in succession Trustees of the Conduit.

The Vicar's Brook commences its course along a channel which is straight enough to show that it is artificial. It is soon joined by another and smaller brook which has issued from the foot of the hill at Granham's nearer to Great Shelford. Some 600 yards from the Nine Wells the Vicar's Brook crosses the ancient parish boundary of Great Shelford, and enters the parish of Trumpington. The Inclosure Award of 1809 for that parish describes the channel at this point, and the description still holds, as follows:

[1] P. 73.

"One public drain, fifteen feet wide at the top, and four feet deep, being the ancient watercourse from Shelford Moor." Then the channel, after crossing the modern boundary of the borough of Cambridge fixed in 1934, passes, at about a mile from the Nine Wells, under the road which is now known as the Long Road, but which fifty years ago was called Mill Road from the windmill which stood at the Trumpington Road end of it. From the Long Road it is only a few hundred yards to the point, just south of the polo ground, where the artificial channel of Hobson's River commences, and from here, for about half a mile as far as to Brooklands Avenue, this artificial channel runs parallel to, and not far away from, the natural Vicar's Brook. Here across a spill-away, by which excess water may be discharged from the artificial channel, a neat bridge of teak has recently been erected on which is recorded the three hundredth anniversary of the death of Hobson in 1631. Then an old iron gateway marks the place where the channel passes out of the ancient parish of Trumpington and into the ancient parish of St Andrew's, Barnwell, and at the same time into the ancient borough of Cambridge. Beyond this gateway the channel skirts the common known as Empty Common. Here, along the west bank of the channel, is a gravel footpath, generally called Finch's Walk from the Charles Finch whose name appears on the back of the obelisk. Alternatively it is called Senior Wrangler's Walk, a name which seems to have arisen through a confusion between Charles Finch

the Mayor and a distinguished mathematician, un-
related to him but of the same name, who was prominent in the town a generation later. On the east bank
is a private garden belonging to the house known
as Brooklands, the owner of which has for many
years been permitted to fill his pond from the watercourse. Along Empty Common Hobson's River is
a parish boundary[1] which is unexpected as parish
boundaries were generally fixed long before the days
of Hobson. The common is held to be part of the
ecclesiastical parish of Little St Mary's, the rest of
which, including Coe Fen, is to the west of the
Trumpington Road. It may be that as the common
had no population, and being common had no rate-
able value, no one troubled to correct an error
originally made by chance. At the end of Empty
Common the channel passes under Brooklands
Avenue. By this point the level of the natural Vicar's
Brook has fallen some ten feet below the level of the
artificial channel, and the Vicar's Brook here turns
away westward. The western end of Brooklands
Avenue was constructed so recently as 1923, previous
to which date it was closed to the public for through
traffic, and was accessible only from the Hills Road
end. This change has facilitated increasing road
traffic, but unfortunately it has detracted from the
rural quiet of Finch's Walk.

From Brooklands Avenue the watercourse is conducted along a raised embankment between Trumpington Road and the University Botanic Garden.

[1] Rowe's map, 1858.

This embankment also carries the side-walk of the Trumpington Road. There is here a spillaway over which superfluous water passes into a pond in the Botanic Garden, a benefit for which the University makes an annual payment to the Trustees. The ducks and swans which add so much to the attractiveness of Hobson's River at this point are visitors from the Botanic Garden, and belong to the University. The road-bridge at Bateman Street was constructed in 1884 by the former Improvement Commissioners of the borough, an *ad hoc* authority which was afterwards absorbed into the Town Council. It was in substitution for a footbridge which had been known as the Whitmore Bridge after Mr George Whitmore who had collected the subscriptions which defrayed the cost of its construction. Mr Whitmore's name is still familiar in Cambridge as it is attached to the business which he established in Downing Street. The channel of Hobson's River then passes through lawns in front of the terrace known as Brookside, opposite to the Leys School. Here it is again at the natural level of the ground, there is no embankment, and the channel has passed out of the valley of the Vicar's Brook. It was in the middle of last century that Brookside was laid out and the terrace built. With its agreeable lawns and fine trees it presents an admirable bit of town planning of an era when town planning was sometimes practised but seldom discussed. The freeholder of each house owns also the freehold of that part of the lawn which is in front of his house, subject to the rights of Hobson's Trustees in the stream and its margins. This does not apply to the narrower lawn and the smaller houses at the north end of the terrace; here the Trustees and the Town Council are responsible. The gravel footpath and the cast-iron railings which are continuous along the whole length of the channel from Finch's Walk to the north end of Brookside seem to have acquired their present form at a single reconstruction, and this seems to have been in the year 1851, for that is the date which may be read on three of the cast-iron bridges which here cross the channel. The name Hurrell on these bridges recalls Swann Hurrell who, in 1847, succeeded his uncle Charles Finch as an ironfounder, and who also served as Mayor.

At the corner of Lensfield Road and Trumpington Road is the conduit head of the system, that is to say, the centre from which the water is distributed over the town. Here the surface-level of the water stands at 39 feet above ordnance datum. From the point where the water issues from the meadow at the Nine Wells there is a fall of $7\frac{3}{4}$ feet down to this conduit head, and provided that the channel is kept properly free from weeds and mud, this fall should be sufficient. Unfortunately the whole fall is completed in the course of the first two miles, and for the last half-mile, from the ancient borough boundary to the conduit head, the channel is nearly level, a circumstance which renders the current rather sluggish along this last stretch of its course.

At the conduit head there now stands a quaint Jacobean structure which, formerly standing on the

Market Hill, was the fountain from which the water was finally delivered to the public. It bears two inscriptions of four lines each; they are not carved, but painted on the plaster. The inscription which faces east, that is, faces away from the Trumpington Road, reads:

Thomas Hobson Carrier between Cambridge and London, a great benefactor to this University Town. Died January 1st 1630 in the 86th year of his age.

That which faces west, that is, faces towards the Trumpington Road, reads:

This structure stood upon the Market Hill and served as a Conduit from 1614 to 1856, in which year it was re-erected on this spot by Public Subscription.

The structure is now adorned with the royal arms. This is unexpected as the Trust has no special connection with the Crown. It is, however, on record how the Town Council, in 1661/2, after the Restoration, ordered that, at a cost of seven pounds, the King's Arms should be set on the Conduit.[1] The Council may have felt that, in view of the very prominent part taken by the member for the borough, Oliver Cromwell, in the recent disturbances, some public exhibition of renewed loyalty was specially necessary from them. The arms now exhibited are not those borne by King Charles II, but are those borne by our more recent monarchs. The Stuart kings and their predecessors quartered the Lilies of France with the Lions of England, a practice which was discontinued during the Napoleonic wars in the reign of George III.

[1] Cooper.

CHAPTER III

THE DISTRIBUTION OF THE WATER
FROM THE CONDUIT HEAD

From the conduit head at Lensfield Corner the water
is distributed over the town by three routes, one down
Trumpington Street, a second to the Market Hill,
and a third to Emmanuel and Christ's Colleges. In
each case there is a fall of eight or nine feet from the
water-level at the conduit head to the level of the
ground outside Pembroke College gateway, on the
Market Hill, and outside Christ's College gateway.

The water is led into Trumpington Street through
a modern glazed pipe to the point where it wells up
into the two well-known runnels which border the
footways along that street. At Pembroke College
gateway the runnels sink again underground and,
turning to the left, the water flows through a modern
drainpipe down Mill Lane, and so into the mill pit.
In front of Addenbrooke's Hospital there is an open
moat full of water. This is what remains of the former
open channel along which the water flowed from the
conduit head to Trumpington Street, but the moat is
now fed from the adjoining runnel in the street.
Down the street north of the hospital there is, in
addition to the two open runnels, a 9 inch glazed
pipe running under the pavement in front of Addenbrooke Place and Fitzwilliam Hall and onwards to a

PLATE II

HOBSON'S CONDUIT *as it stood previous to 1856 on the Market Hill*

point just short of the chapel of Pembroke College where it turns to the right and, passing through the college grounds, emerges into Pembroke Street near Free School Lane. Formerly this line ran on into the old Botanic Garden, but it was turned off into the public sewers in 1886, when laboratories were built over the disused garden.

From the conduit head to the Market Hill there is a line of iron pipes. After crossing Lensfield Road this line runs through the gardens behind the houses in Bene't Place and in Trumpington Street, then down Tennis Court Road behind Addenbrooke's Hospital, across St Andrew's Hill, down Guildhall Place, and so to the Market Hill. The pressure in the pipes is sufficient to deliver the water there at a height of three or four feet above ground-level. The fountain which now stands in the centre of the Market Hill was erected by the Town Council, not the Trustees, some eighty years ago when the old fountain, or Conduit, was removed to Lensfield Corner. This new fountain is adorned with statues of eight natives of the town, including Thomas Hobson,[1] but the sculptor has not succeeded in producing a representation of Hobson which is readily recognizable by those who frequent the Market Hill. Certain coats of arms of local interest, including those of Dr Andrew Perne of Peterhouse, are also carved on the fountain.

On the Market Hill there is a branch pipe line which leads to a point on the footpath close to the

[1] Cooper, 1856.

south-east corner of Great St Mary's Church and close to the shop, No. 30, now occupied by Messrs Barrett. Within living memory there was a dipping-hole at this point. Water could be drawn from it by lifting a stone cover and lowering a pail. Although the dipping-hole has vanished from the public foot-path, yet Messrs Barrett close by are still able to draw Hobson's water for their private use out of a tap in their basement.

A third channel leads off from the conduit head. This passes down Lensfield Road to the Roman Catholic Church at Hyde Park Corner, at first in a brick culvert under the front gardens of Downing Terrace, and then in a modern two-foot glazed pipe. This stretch from Downing Terrace to Hyde Park Corner was formerly an open uncovered watercourse like that which now runs in front of the Botanic Garden, but in the 'seventies of last century it was said to be dangerous for children and was covered over, and a wide footpath was made above it. At Hyde Park Corner the water passes under Hills Road into the corner site recently acquired by the Perse School, then northwards under the road, under Regent Terrace, and along the backs of those houses which occupy the narrow strip between Regent Street and Parker's Piece. At the north end of this strip close to the University Arms Hotel, on the boundary of the ground occupied by the shop now known as Regent House, there was formerly one of the dipping-holes, and from this point a branch pipe slanted across the road to supply the old Hobson's workhouse which stood on the other side. The water then runs under the pavement in front of the University Arms Hotel, and so on down Regent and St Andrew's Street until it reaches Emmanuel College. Here the main stream turns to the right and enters the college grounds, but the surplus water goes straight on and, welling up in St Andrew's Street, runs in two open runnels down either side of the street until, opposite the gate of Christ's College, it is swallowed up into a public drain. The main stream which turns into the grounds of Emmanuel College first feeds the pond in the smaller college garden called Chapman's Garden, and then, passing under some college buildings which were erected in 1633, two years after the construction of this watercourse, feeds both the larger college pond and the college bathing pool. The pool owes its present form and character to a reconstruction effected in 1845 by the then bursar of the college, the Rev. William Castlehow, whose name may be read on the concrete bottom of the pool when it is emptied for cleaning. It is because Hobson's water has been available that these two ponds and the bathing pool have been able to give to the college grounds their characteristic beauty. Within the college grounds the channel is not piped but runs in a brick-arched covered drain. Near the Drummer Street wall is a dipping-hole which is a good surviving example of the dipping-holes out of which the public formerly drew water in the streets outside.

From the larger pond in the garden of Emmanuel College the water passes out north-eastward into

Drummer Street, and turning to the left runs under this street right up to the garden wall of Christ's College. On this section of its course under Drummer Street the old brick-arched drain was replaced at least fifty years ago by a 12-inch glazed pipe. From the point where Drummer Street meets the garden wall of Christ's College there is, firstly, a leaden pipe which leads straight on through the wall, and leaving the Fellows' Building to the northward, brings water to the Master's Lodge, and secondly, an iron pipe which turns to the right, continues for a short space under Milton's Walk outside the college grounds, and then passes under the wall into the Fellows' Garden. The first pipe now fills an ornamental pond which was designed in the Master's Garden by a late Master, Dr Shipley. The second pipe, after passing through several dipping-holes in the Fellows' Garden, fills the college bathing pool. This bathing pool is adorned with a funeral urn commemorating Dr Meade and with busts of John Milton and other distinguished members of the college. Recently the pool has become known beyond the confines of the college through an imaginative story entitled *A College Mystery*, written by the late A. P. Baker of this college, and published in 1918. There is also at this college a brick-arched drain, still existing but now disused, which formerly led the surplus water from the point where the water enters the college along a line under the screens and under the principal gateway of the college, and discharged, originally no doubt into the King's Ditch, but now into a public drain. The water which issues from the bathing pool emerges from the Fellows' Garden on to Milton's Walk where the trace of a former dipping-hole may be seen. The water now goes on into a public drain.

Those who designed and constructed this third outfall from the conduit head had to contend with the difficulty that the fall was slight. From the conduit head to Emmanuel College the road surface along Lensfield Road and Regent Street is perfectly level, so that there is only so much fall for the water as can be contrived by digging the ditch, or burying the pipe, deeper at the end of the course than at the beginning. After the water has reached Emmanuel College the difficulties are less, for from that college the fall to Christ's College and to King Street is appreciable.

CHAPTER IV

THE ELIZABETHAN PROPOSALS

The written history of the Cambridge New River begins in 1574. There is extant a plan of Cambridge of that date made by one Richard Lyne. A note in the Latin language on the margin of the plan runs as follows:[1]

Henry III, King of England, about the year 1265 fortified Cambridge with a ditch and gates. At this time he was defending himself against rebel outlaws who occupied the Isle of Ely. He would have surrounded the town again with a wall, but Gilbert, Earl of Clare, occupied London in his absence, so that he was compelled to divert his attention to this new difficulty. From that time the ditch has been called the King's Ditch, and the line of it is to be seen on this map. But the Ditch which was at first constructed with wide and deep trenchings in order to surround the town and defend it, now serves, and not badly, for carrying off the sewage and for washing away ordure into the River Granta. But if Cambridge people would subscribe of their resources, and would arrange so that the stream which there is at the ford of Trumpington should flush out the Ditch, there would then be no town pleasanter than Cambridge. The recollection of such a work would not only be pleasant and useful to those now living, but also agreeable to those who come after us.

The Gilbert, Earl of Clare, who is mentioned here by Lyne, is the ninth earl, called the Red Earl. He

[1] Willis and Clark, vol. i, p. xcvii.

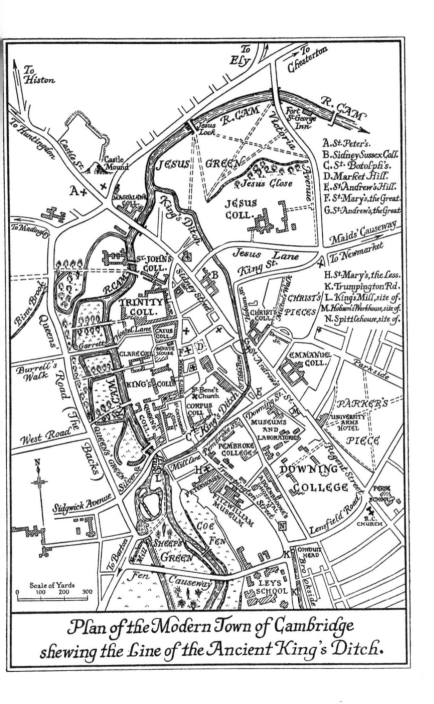

A. St. Peter's.
B. Sidney Sussex Coll.
C. St. Botolph's.
D. Market Hill.
E. St. Andrew's Hill.
F. St. Mary's, the Great.
G. St. Andrew's, the Great.

Maids' Causeway

H. St. Mary's, the Less.
K. Trumpington Rd.
L. King's Mill, site of.
M. Hobson's Workhouse, site of.
N. Spittlehouse, site of.

Plan of the Modern Town of Cambridge
shewing the Line of the Ancient King's Ditch.

was the father of Elizabeth, the foundress of Clare College.

Lyne's plan of Cambridge was attached to *De Antiquitate*, a history of Cambridge which was written by Dr Keyes, or Caius (1510–73), the Master and second founder of Gonville and Caius College. Dr Keyes was a physician, and not only was he a physician, but also, which is important here, he was a sanitarian, interested in that aspect of medical science which is now called public health. Thus in the college court which he constructed, he broke with tradition, in that, having built three sides, he left the south side unbuilt and open, and his reason which he has recorded was "lest the air from being confined to a narrow space should become foul",[1] and he also left directions as to the cleansing of the pavements and as to imposing fines as a penalty for scattering rubbish. It may be supposed that the opinion expressed on Lyne's map was inspired by Dr Keyes, and in a matter so closely concerning the public health as the flushing out of the King's Ditch, the opinion of Dr Keyes would have carried weight.

There is preserved also a relevant letter, written in the same year, 1574, by Dr Perne, Master of Peterhouse and Vice-Chancellor of the University, to Lord Burghley, the Chancellor.[2] Dr Perne is reporting on an outbreak of plague at Cambridge from which more than one hundred persons had died. He piously confesses, using the thought and expres-

[1] *Cambridge Described and Illustrated*, by Atkinson and Clark, 1897.
[2] Cooper.

sion of his time, that our sinfulness is the principal
cause of this as of all other plagues sent by Almighty
God. But he goes on to say that the secondary cause
is not the corruption of the air as the physicians say,
but is partly the clothing of a certain Londoner who
brought the plague to Cambridge, and is partly the
corruption of the King's Ditch which goeth through
Cambridge, and he ends his letter by saying that he
encloses a map to show how the stream which comes
from Shelford to Trumpington Ford might be conveyed from this ford to the King's Ditch for the
perpetual scouring of the same, which would be a
benefit to the health of both University and Town,
as well as otherwise useful.

Of this correspondence between Dr Perne and
Lord Burghley we have one further letter, that which
is printed in Appendix III, p. 126. The date written
upon it is 18 January 1574, which in our modern
style under which the new year begins on 1 January
would be 1575. In it Dr Perne reports the progress
of the plague, complains of the slowness of the
Mayor to cleanse the King's Ditch and the streets of
the town, and sends up for the Chancellor's opinion
two reports on the project for leading the water from
Trumpington Ford into the King's Ditch and two
tenders for the work, one from a certain Richard
Browne who is described alternatively as a Workman,
and as the Keeper of the Water Mills at Lynn, and
the other from a John Bryant of Cambridge. It will
be observed that these reports and tenders are from
practical men and not from professors of mathe-

matics. The Mayor in 1574 was Thomas Kimbolde, this being his third term of office. He died in 1603 and is buried in St Sepulchre's Church. Roger Slegge, whom Dr Perne mentions, was several times Mayor and represented the borough in Parliament. In the sixteenth century the relations between the Town and the University were the reverse of cordial, and Roger Slegge was the leader of the Town in its contests with the University, Thomas Kimbolde being one of his party. It may be supposed that Dr Perne, in writing thus to Lord Burghley, was angling for his support in the perennial contest between the University and the Town.

Dr Perne, Master of Peterhouse (1554–89), was a notable man. His fine library is still one of the treasures of his college. But he held his mastership continuously through the religious changes of the reigns of Edward VI, Mary and Elizabeth, so that his friends, while conscious of the wisdom of his leadership, were hesitant in their appreciation of his honesty. The letters A P, properly referring to St Andrew and St Peter, may still be read on the weathercock of St Peter's Church on Castle Hill. In the days when Perne was still remembered, the public, naturally though erroneously associating this church with this college, whispered the mocking story that it was in memory of Dr Perne that the weathercock had been erected, and that the letters A P stood equally for "Andrew Perne", "A Papist", "A Puritan" or "A Protestant". Dr Perne was a man of tolerant temper who lived in an intolerant generation.

Another candidate for the distinction of being the first to project the construction of the Cambridge New River is Archbishop Matthew Parker (1504–1575), who in earlier life had been Master of Corpus Christi College. It is certain that the archbishop as well as John Caius were in close touch with Lyne the mapmaker, for Lyne has engraved the archbishop's arms on his map, and moreover a certain Richard Parker (1572–1629), a fellow of Caius College, writing in 1622, makes this claim, explicitly, on behalf of his distinguished namesake.[1]

It is unlikely that the proposal for the construction of this Cambridge New River originated with any one man alone to the exclusion of others; it would naturally have taken shape as a result of general discussion amongst the leading men of the University and Town. At that date waterworks were nothing new or unusual. At Plymouth Sir Francis Drake's New River, or Leat as it was called locally, had been inaugurated as recently as 1591, and, far more important to Cambridge people, Londoners were actively discussing their water supply, and were framing the scheme which resulted in the construction of the Ware to London New River in the following reign contemporaneously with the construction of the Cambridge New River. These London discussions were the more important to Cambridge in that Cambridge men of that date passed through Ware on their journey to London. Nowadays there are three

[1] Σκελετός Cantabrigiensis, by Parker, printed by Hearne in 1715 in Vol. v of John Leland's *Collectanea*.

principal roads from Cambridge to London, the Great North Road by Baldock, the Old North Road by Ware, and the road by Bishop's Stortford and Epping, but the Great North Road did not come into prominence until the days of stage coaches and Turnpike Acts in the eighteenth century, and the way through Bishop's Stortford and Epping is across a heavy clay country which would have been often founderous before the days of McAdam and of substantial roadmaking. On the other hand the Old North Road by Ware across Hertfordshire is over dry chalk country, and moreover it was one of the chief roads in the kingdom, so that even if unsurfaced according to our modern standards, it must have been better cared for than other roads; indeed further north its bridge at Huntingdon was so good that it is in use to this day. The preoccupation of the traveller from Cambridge to London was the point at which he should join the Old North Road; in wet weather he would ride by Barton to Wimpole rather than by Fowlmere to Puckeridge so as to join the Old North Road without crossing any stream of importance, but whether he joined it at Puckeridge, Royston, Wimpole or Caxton, he would necessarily pass through Ware on his way on to London. This was before the days of stage coaches, and the traveller on horseback would have generally taken two days over the journey, as Samuel Pepys, also on horseback, used to do a hundred years later. In the inn at Ware where they stayed the night they would discuss the project for the Ware to London New River which was being planned to run, as it now runs, alongside the high-road. Thus Cambridge people who, in the days of Queen Elizabeth, conceived the project of the Cambridge New River, were well acquainted with the project for the Ware to London New River.

It is unlikely that Hobson was the first to conceive and to promote the scheme for the construction of the Cambridge New River, even although his name was afterwards given to it, for when, in 1574, Dr Perne was expounding the scheme Hobson, though already at work as a carrier, was only thirty years of age, and cannot have attained the influential position in the town which he held in later life. Nevertheless, it is quite likely that as Hobson was continually on the London Road, Dr Keyes, Dr Perne and their friends habitually came to him to hear what was being planned and done at Ware.

CHAPTER V

THE ANCIENT KING'S DITCH

To the Elizabethans, the objective, for the sake of which the Cambridge New River was to be constructed, was the perpetual scouring out of the King's Ditch. The supply of better drinking water for the town was not excluded as a secondary objective, but it was not explicitly mentioned in the earliest documents. It is necessary therefore to consider what the King's Ditch was in the days of Queen Elizabeth.

The line of the Ditch is well known. Starting from the mill pit below the King's Mill, it followed along Mill Lane and Pembroke Street, passed across the site of the old Botanic Garden, then under the site of the modern Masonic Hall, along St Tibb's Row, and then, leaving Great St Andrew's Church just outside the town, along Hobson Street, across the garden of Sidney Sussex College, along Park Street, and so into the River Cam just above Jesus Green and opposite to the Pepysian Library at Magdalene College. In earlier days it had been bridged and gated opposite to Pembroke and Christ's Colleges, but as there is no trace nor record of any brick or stone gate there, it may be supposed that these constructions were of timber. A town ditch was a cheap

alternative to a town wall, and a medieval town
needed some such barrier, not for military purposes
only, but also for police purposes so that it could be
known who had gone in and out of the town. It is
not known whether the gates still existed in the days
of Queen Elizabeth. Originally the Ditch had been
so traced as to include within it nearly all the houses
of the town; afterwards, as the town grew, buildings were erected outside of it, so that by the year
1574 it was no longer running round the town
but, as Dr Perne says, it was running through the
town.

That rubbish and filth were thrown into it, and
that foul sewers were discharged into it, is inherently
likely, and is confirmed by Dr Perne's complaint of
the corruption of the Ditch. As more houses came to
be built outside as well as inside the line of the Ditch
its corruption was intensified, and at the same time
the number of people who were near enough to be
annoyed by this corruption was increased.

It must be supposed that at one time the Ditch had
been, for the whole of its length, wide and deep so as
to be an effective military obstacle, but that was no
longer so in the days of Queen Elizabeth. As many
as three separate maps made during that reign have
survived, one by Lyne dated 1574, one by Braun
dated 1575, and one by Hamond dated 1592. In
these maps the King's Ditch is shown as being still,
for a great part of its length, an important feature of
the ground. It is well marked from the corner where
Free School Lane meets Pembroke Street, eastwards

and northwards, by St Tibb's Row and across Sidney College garden to the river at Jesus Green. It is well marked too, especially by Hamond, along the length of Mill Lane where it is crossed by two foot-bridges. But from Free School Lane to Trumpington Street it is not shown at all, which suggests that already along that part of its length it was arched over, or filled in, or so nearly filled in as to be negligible.

It has been observed that the course of the King's Ditch follows along the natural outfall of the water which issues from the gravel beds on the east of the town,[1] but this is not very important, for the flow of water from these gravel beds would have been intermittent, and the volume inconsiderable. As a military obstacle the Ditch must have been originally conceived as a dry moat, or at least as one in which the water, when there was any, was of no military importance.

It cannot be supposed that the waters of the River Cam ever flowed freely through the Ditch, entering from the mill pit and discharging again into the river at Jesus Green. The levels of land and water would not admit of it to-day, and it is likely that the levels were much the same in the sixteenth century as in the twentieth. There are indeed some areas of land in the town which have been raised and consolidated by human agency since the Ditch was dug. These are areas very near to the River Cam which were originally mere river marsh. But there is also the

[1] T. McK. Hughes, C.A.S. 1914, vol. XIX.

ridge of relatively high ground along which the
Trumpington Road and the Hills Road led northwards to the Great Bridge below Castle Hill, and this
ridge has always existed. It is on account of this line
of high ground and of the practicable river crossing
thereby created that the town of Cambridge first
rose to importance. The line of the King's Ditch
crosses this line of high ground at the old Botanic
Garden and at the modern Masonic Hall behind
St Andrew's Hill. Modern builders and roadmakers
may have raised the ground-level here, but not by
more than a foot or two. At this high point of its
course the Ditch may have been dug very deep, but it
can hardly have been dug so deep that its bed here
was as low as the normal water-level of the mill
pit.

The water-level too at which the river water stood
in the mill pit must have been much the same in the
days of Queen Elizabeth as it is to-day. It has indeed
been argued on the evidence of some old submerged
quays that the normal level of the water was formerly
lower, as much as four feet lower, than it is to-day,
but that evidence is better explained by the sinking
of these ancient quays into the soft mud. To our predecessors the consideration which was of paramount
importance was the need to maintain a sufficient
depth of water, say three or four feet, to float their
barges round the Backs of the Colleges and up to the
mill pit; they would not therefore have permitted
the water to stand at a lower level than at present. In
1639 at a Session of the Sewers holden at the

Guildhall it was ordered that all colleges, especially Queens' College, shall have notice to scour and deepen their rivers so that boats may pass into the mill dam as formerly they have.[1] To-day the level of the river water at the mill pit and round the Backs through the town depends on Jesus Lock. This lock is only one hundred years old, but it was preceded by the Cambridge Sluice[2] which stood where the Fort St George Inn now stands, only a couple of hundred yards lower down the river, and indeed as far back as 1578 it is recorded[3] that there was something of a weir at this point. It appears too from Ackerman's series of pictures of Cambridge which were published in 1815, that at that date the water on the Backs stood against the college bridges and lawns at the same level as to-day. Moreover the architectural features of the college bridges, some of which date as far back as the seventeenth century, were designed for a water-level much the same as the water-level of to-day. Lastly, the belief that the levels of land and water in the sixteenth and in the twentieth centuries were the same obtains some confirmation from the enclosures to Dr Perne's letter of 18 January 1574/5 to the Chancellor. (Appendix III.)

The water of the mill stream above the King's Mill does indeed stand some five feet higher than the water in the mill pit below, but the Ditch took off from below and not from above the mill; that is clear

[1] C.A.S. vol. xiv, 1910, "Old Mills of Cambridge", by Stokes.
[2] *Cambridge*, by Le Keux, 1841, map.
[3] Cooper.

from the contemporary maps. And irrespective of the evidence of the maps the total water-power available is not great, so little power is there that at one time the several mills could not all work simultaneously.[1] The millers would therefore have objected if it had ever been proposed to draw water into the King's Ditch out of the mill stream above the mill, for that would have caused a considerable loss of power to them.

It can confidently be assumed that neither in the sixteenth century nor at any other time was the King's Ditch habitually scoured out by any natural flow through it of the waters of the River Cam.

The thorough way to deal with the corruption of the Ditch was to fill it up or cover it in, so as to make it impossible for the neighbours to defile it any more, and to order the adjoining householders to cart their rubbish and filth to a distance. But no doubt many householders claimed a prescriptive right to use the Ditch as a cess pit, and valued the convenience because it was cheap.

In respect of public sanitation and town cleansing the position in Elizabethan England recalls the position in India forty years ago before the discoveries of Sir Ronald Ross. At that date the Indian officials perceived, but as yet only dimly, that stagnant pools of water were a cause of malaria, but they were not sufficiently confident in that opinion to face the expense and the unpopularity of filling up those pools. Equally in Dr Perne's day, while men of

[1] C.A.S. vol. XIV, 1910, "Old Mills of Cambridge", by Stokes.

education were beginning to perceive that bad town cleansing was one important cause of disease, their knowledge had not then reached that point of certainty which was necessary before the governing authorities would think it to be worth while to face the unpopularity of insisting on expensive sanitary measures, of the ultimate efficacy of which the public were doubtful or even incredulous.

CHAPTER VI

THE WATER BROUGHT DOWN TRUMPINGTON STREET TO THE KING'S DITCH

The most important contribution to our knowledge of the construction of the Conduit is a deed dated 26 October 1610 in which the Lord of the Manor of Trumpington Delapole, Thomas Chaplyn, agrees with the University and Town jointly that they should conduct the water from the Nine Wells across the parish and common fields of Trumpington, diverting much of it away from its natural course down the Vicar's Brook.[1] In connection with the parish of Trumpington there are at least two manors, but so far as is here material the manor of Trumpington Delapole is conterminous with the parish of Trumpington. This deed tells us that the watercourse had then been newly and lately made. It recites how the current had been led, ultimately, through the common drain or sewer called the King's Ditch into the river and high stream there. The object is stated to be to scour and cleanse the drain and ditch abovementioned by the water running continually, or for the most part, through the same, and also for the cleansing of divers drains and watercourses belonging to divers and sundry colleges and halls and houses of students within the University. The supply of drink-

[1] Cooper.

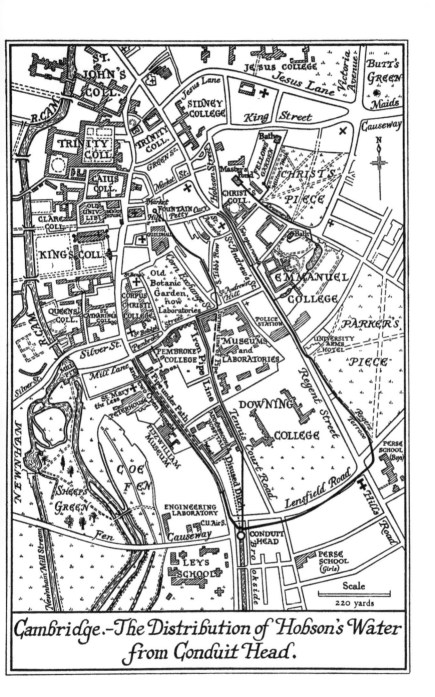

Cambridge.—The Distribution of Hobson's Water from Conduit Head.

ing water is not mentioned in this deed as being one of the principal objects of these first constructors. The deed does refer in general terms to the health and welfare of the people of both bodies, that is, both the University and the Town, but broadly speaking its language is regardful more particularly of the needs of the University.

The design of this Cambridge New River has been attributed to a distinguished contemporary Cambridge mathematician; it has been stated more than once that the plan was Edward Wright's, who was M.A. of Caius College, and the best mathematician of his day, and gave also to Sir Hugh Middleton the plan of his New River.[1] Edward Wright (1558–1615) was the mathematician who put the art of navigation on a scientific basis. With personal experience of seamanship he published in 1599 a book entitled *Certain Errors in Navigation Detected and Corrected*. He discusses the fact that the lines of longitude are fewer miles apart in high than in low latitudes, his work being part of that body of thought which led to the construction of maps and charts on the system known as Mercator's projection.[2] But in fact many lesser men than Edward Wright were quite capable of laying out the course of the New River. It was to one Richard Browne who is described as Keeper of the Water Mills at Lynn, and not to a University professor of mathematics, that Dr Perne referred to in 1575. (Appendix III.)

[1] *Cambridge Portfolio*, by Smith, 1840.
[2] *History of Mathematics at Cambridge*, by Rouse Ball, 1889.

In connection with the Ware to London New River it is recorded that one of the greatest difficulties was the prevention of leakage from an artificially raised watercourse, and the constructors of the Cambridge New River must have experienced the same difficulty. The prevention of leakage from a raised canal is, even in our own day, a matter of trial and error. Puddling is a matter for the practical man, as distinguished from the laying out of the line of a canal which may need an instructed surveyor with some knowledge of mathematics. There would have been men to be had from Ely and the fens who had had some experience of raised canal banks, but in 1610 the great fund of experience amassed in this country during the construction of the great navigation canals of the eighteenth century was not yet available. On the Cambridge New River the watercourse along the length of Empty Common is above the level of the natural Vicar's Brook close by, and between the new Botanic Garden and the Trumpington Road it is carried on an embankment which is several feet above the ground on either side. The prevention of leakage depends on finding a good puddling clay. At Ely the Kimmeridge beds of clay have been and are still being used for puddling the banks of the rivers and lodes of the fens.[1] Kimmeridge clay is to be had at Cambridge, but the stiff blue clay known as gault may well have been preferred. Gault is the clay out of which the yellow bricks, so familiar in Cambridge, were made at Barnwell, and it

[1] *Geology of Cambridgeshire*, by Cowper Reed, 1897, p. 43.

comes to the surface along a line from Barnwell brickpits right up to the east end of Brooklands Avenue, a point which is very near to the raised channel of Hobson's River. The constructors had therefore a supply of good puddling clay quite near at hand.

The principal objective in 1610 being the flushing out of the King's Ditch, the water, having arrived at the conduit head, was led northwards across Lensfield Road, behind the old almshouses of St Anthony and St Eligius, across the site on which Addenbrooke's Hospital has since been erected, and then in a single stream down the middle or nearly the middle of Trumpington Street as far as the cross-road at the gate of Pembroke College where it fell into the King's Ditch. From that point the water turned to the left, westwards, down Mill Lane, and flushed out, no doubt efficiently, that length of the King's Ditch, either the old open Ditch itself or some covered drain by which perhaps it may have already been replaced. But the length of Mill Lane is short, and by far the greater length of the Ditch is that which extended from Trumpington Street eastwards up Pembroke Street and beyond. It is not known whether the constructors expected that the water would run along this eastward portion, nor whether in fact it did so run. The levels of Pembroke Street and of the old Botanic Garden where the course of the Ditch lies may have been raised as much as a foot or two in recent years by roadmakers and builders, but the level of the surface of Trumpington Street is fixed by

the gateway of Pembroke College which has stood
there unaltered since before 1610. The surface-level
along Pembroke Street eastwards from Trumpington
Street must always have been uphill and, at the most,
the Ditch was not dug more than three or four feet
deep at the old Botanic Garden; that seems certain
from a report of twenty years later by a Mr Bond.[1]
It is therefore unlikely that Hobson's water coming
from Trumpington Street ever effectively flushed out
the longer length eastwards of the King's Ditch.

There was, however, a subsidiary channel which
took off from this Trumpington Street channel
opposite Little St Mary's Church, and which, passing
round the back of the buildings of Pembroke College
as they existed in 1610, crossed Pembroke Street and
fell into the King's Ditch a little west of Free School
Lane. It is not known whether this was a part of the
original plan of 1610, or whether it was constructed
at a later date because it was found that the water
would not run freely up Pembroke Street. It is
known that it existed in 1688.[2] It passes underneath college buildings which were erected in 1633
and in 1659, which circumstance so far as it goes
tends to the conclusion that the channel is older
than those two buildings. This channel, passing
under the present Fellows' Combination Room,
crosses the New Court of the college from south to
north, and its course there, though now piped, was
until modern times an open ditch. It has been

[1] P. 41.
[2] Loggan's map.

claimed that it was the celebrated divine, Dr Lancelot Andrewes, who arranged for the construction of this subsidiary channel,[1] but although Dr Andrewes lived until 1626 his mastership of Pembroke College ended in 1605, before the construction of the Conduit.

In the eighteenth century Pembroke College made much use of the water thus brought to them. Carter, writing in 1753 of the Master's Lodge,[2] says:

> But the chief beauty of this lodge is (in my opinion) the gardens, and therein the waterworks contrived by the present master (and here let me tell you that he is a very great mechanic), which supplies a beautiful and large bason in the middle of the garden and wherein he often diverts himself in a machine of his own contrivance, to go with the foot as he rides therein.

And Carter continues with reference to the Fellows' Garden:

> There are besides several other gardens belonging to the apartments of particular fellows, in one of which is another, small and simple, yet well-contrived waterwork which is continually supplying a large cold bath with fresh water, the overplus of which runs through the second court and so into the King's Ditch.

The Master to whom Carter here refers was Dr Roger Long, Lowndes Professor of Astronomy. The garden of the Master's Lodge then lay on the south side of the chapel and the dining hall. The apartment of a particular fellow in connection with which a large

---

[1] *Pembroke College*, by Attwater, 1937, p. 56.
[2] *History of the University of Cambridge*, by Carter, 1753.

cold bath was contrived was the room now used as a Fellows' Combination Room which until recently consisted of a set of residential rooms, dayroom, bedroom, etc. In the bedroom floor was a trap-door which, though it had been screwed down for many years, had formerly given access to a basement in which the cold bath was situated, being fed by the watercourse which flowed past it.

As to whether or no this scheme for the scouring out of the King's Ditch was successful in that aim there is some conflict of evidence. So far as the length of Mill Lane is concerned the enterprise was a success; there is no reason to doubt that. But in respect of the longer part of the Ditch, from Pembroke Street eastwards and northwards to Sidney Sussex College and to Jesus Green, it is not at all certain that this scouring out of the Ditch was effective. Some water was led into the highest part of the Ditch in the old Botanic Garden. We have written evidence that this was so in 1842,[1] and so presumably it was done from the first, but it does not follow that the volume of water was enough to effect a real scouring out of the Ditch.

Fuller, writing in 1655, acclaimed the scheme as a success. He said of the Ditch:

in our fathers' days filled up with filth and mire, what was made for the fortifying, became a great annoying to the University until some 50 years since, partly at the cost of Dr James Montague (Master of Sidney College, afterwards Bishop of Winchester) a rivulet was let into the same: so

[1] P. 111.

not only clearing it, but turning the annoyance into a great conveniency of water to some colleges and to the town in general.[1]

Fuller's evidence is the more important because he was for a time specially connected with Sidney Sussex College, whence in 1635 he took his B.D. degree. The Rev. William Cole, the local eighteenth-century diarist, also believed that the scheme had been a success, but he wrote as late as 1748. Cole says, referring to Dr Montague:

for the King's Ditch in Cambridge being at that time very offensive to the Inhabitants he at the expence of an Hundred Pounds brought a clear running Water into it, to the no small Conveniency and Pleasure both of the Town and University.[2]

On the other hand in such seventeenth-century accounts for Sidney Sussex College as have been preserved there are some entries of payments for the cleansing of the Ditch. The entries which have survived are sufficiently numerous to suggest to us that the current was not then flowing along the Ditch continuously and in sufficient volume to be altogether effective. There is extant also a very interesting drawing of a technical and professional character dated 1629 and made by a surveyor of the name of Bond or Pond.[3] It is designed to show the levels of the King's Ditch at different points along its course from Pembroke

[1] *History of Cambridge University to 1614*, by Fuller, written 1655, ed. Prickett and Wright, 1840.

[2] Willis and Clark, vol. II, p. 739.

[3] C.A.S. vol. XI, p. 251; and Univ. Registry, bound vol. Commons, etc. 3. A. 4, no. 76.

Hall to Jesus Green. The surveyor claims that there is a fall of 15 feet along this course, but he complains that the fall is irregular, first steep, then level for a bit, and in places even uphill. He asks for a steady and regular fall, equal along the whole length. He gives the width of the Ditch as varying from 20 to 54 inches, being 3 or 4 feet wide along the greater part of its course. This is unexpectedly narrow: the Ditch was much diminished since the days when Henry III thought to make it of military value for the defence of the town. It was perhaps Bond's report which supplied the inspiration for the order for the improvement of the Ditch with which the Order of the Court of Sewers of 23 April 1634 (Appendix IV) concludes, but we have no evidence that any effective action was taken. Bond's report clearly indicates that the flush of water was not then carrying away all the filth which fell into the Ditch, and while Fuller, an historian, might have permitted his words to be coloured by a momentary optimism, Bond's report is the considered report of a professional man. Indeed, the fact that a professional man was asked to make a report is of itself evidence that something was wrong.

Even if a partial success was at first attained, that measure of success must have been reduced when, as hereafter related, some of the water which was at first poured into the Ditch was diverted to the Market Hill and to Christ's and Emmanuel Colleges. But these two colleges were to permit their surplus water to run away, mostly by way of the St Andrew's

Street runnels, into the King's Ditch at Christ's College gateway, from which point it would flow along the Ditch north-eastwards by Hobson Street, across the garden of Sidney Sussex College, and to the river at Jesus Green. The difference between Bond's condemnation and Fuller's appreciation may perhaps be partially bridged by the supposition that, although the first flushing of the Ditch by way of Trumpington Street was an indifferent success justifying Bond's report, yet afterwards the water which came by way of Lensfield Road and Emmanuel College and was poured into the Ditch at Christ's College gate was enough to flush the Ditch from that point onwards, and to justify the more favourable character of Fuller's subsequent report.

But, irrespective of any written evidence, the undertaking, designed for the flushing out of the King's Ditch, lies before us so that modern experts in waterworks engineering should be able to say how far it is likely to have been effective. The total volume of the water was not great, assuming it to have been the same as it was forty years ago before the Water Company began to pump the water out of the chalk uplands of the Gog Magog Hills. The gradients too are slight, and moreover water would flow less freely down the old irregular brick-lined, or merely earthen, ditches than it flows down the concreted channels or the glazed pipes of to-day. It may be that, in order to flush out the Ditch effectively, the conduit head, instead of being placed at Lensfield Corner, ought to have been carried on to St Andrew's Hill, whence the water could have been poured directly into the highest part of the Ditch.

It is, too, quite likely that the public discussion about the construction of the New River and the flushing out of the Ditch resulted in the growth of a wiser public opinion which was desirous that the Ditch should be clean, and which was more ready to submit to regulations restrictive of its use as a cesspit. In that case the need for the flush would have become less urgent as years went by.

CHAPTER VII

THE WATER BROUGHT TO THE MARKET HILL

After the first construction of the New River to the conduit head and down Trumpington Street to the King's Ditch, the next step in the development of the system was that taken in 1614 when the water was brought by pipes from the conduit head to the Market Hill, to a conduit erected there of stone and fitted with a lead cistern. This was done at the joint charge of the University and Town. The payments to meet this expenditure were not made very promptly, for in 1620 there was a complaint that the contractors had not been fully paid as the inhabitants do either deny or else have very slenderly contributed to those who have so perfected the said work,[1] and in 1622 the Privy Council enjoined proceedings against those inhabitants who had not paid the assessments set upon them.[2] The pipes were leaden pipes[3] and so remained until 1842. They may not have been fit to stand any great pressure, but apparently on arrival at the Market Hill the water was ready to rise in them some six or eight feet. The line of the pipes crossed the King's Ditch but made no

[1] Cooper.

[2] *Acts of the Privy Council, 1621–23*, published 1832, p. 339.

[3] Carter's *Cambridgeshire*, 1753; and Lysons' *Cambridgeshire*, 1810, p. 141.

connection with it. While there may be some doubt
whether the flushing out of the King's Ditch ever
was a success, there can be none about the success of this scheme which brought pure drinking
water into the centre of the town. This was of great
value for two hundred and fifty years until the construction of a modern steam-pumped waterworks.

Now the name of Hobson, the carrier, has been
attached to the Cambridge New River since the early
days of its history. John Evelyn, the diarist, visiting
Cambridge in 1654, only twenty-three years after
Hobson's death, wrote of the Market Hill that it was
remarkable for old Hobson's, the pleasant carrier's,
beneficence of a fountain. But many people have
thought that in speaking of Hobson's conduit,
Hobson's fountain and of Hobson's river, credit is
being given to Hobson which is not properly due to
him. It is the case that on his death in 1631 Hobson
bequeathed property for the upkeep of the watercourse, some of it being earmarked for the improvement of the fountain on Market Hill, but such
written evidence as survives certainly fails to indicate
Hobson as a principal promoter of the original undertaking, and, although it gives no clear indication of
any other particular person as taking the lead in the
matter, yet it leaves the impression that the original
undertaking of 1610 was pushed more by members
of the University than by Hobson or any other
townsman. Recently the local historians of Plymouth
have advanced the theory that Sir Francis Drake was
not the charitable donor of a waterworks to his town,

as he has been acclaimed to be for three hundred years, but that he was merely the contractor who as a matter of business constructed it for the corporation. It is not impossible that in the same way Hobson was the contractor who undertook the construction of the Cambridge New River as a matter of business and for his own profit. Such an assumption would account for the connection of his name with the watercourse, but there is no evidence that Hobson was accustomed to undertake contracts of this character, and against it we have the fact that his testamentary attitude towards the undertaking was a charitable attitude, not quite in keeping with a connection of a predominantly business character. Moreover by the year 1610 Hobson was already well over sixty years of age, well established in life, and one of the rich men of the town, so that although he was well able to be a charitable subscriber he had no need to undertake contracts.

On this point Bowtell (1753–1813), antiquary and bookbinder of Trinity Street, writes:

Whilst the University and the Corporation were employed in forwarding the work of this little river, the ever memorable Hobson formed the design of carrying the water through leaden pipes from the Spittle-House to the centre of the town, where a conduit was erected at his expense in 1614.[1]

Bowtell is mistaken if he means that Hobson bore the whole expense of erecting the fountain, but the

[1] C.A.S. vol. XLVII, 1915, p. 41, "Cambridge Outside the Barnwell Gate", by Stokes.

tradition which Bowtell thus records that Hobson took the lead in the supplementary undertaking of piping the water from the conduit head to the Market Hill may well be a near version of the facts. It can, too, be understood how the townspeople who were conscious of the benefit of pure drinking water on Market Hill, but forgetful of or indifferent to the cleansing of the King's Ditch, would come to attribute the whole water system to the man who was assumed to have brought the water to the Market Hill. Perse and Potto were early benefactors of the watercourse as well as Hobson, and yet their contemporaries chose Hobson's name as the name of the Conduit, thus attributing the enterprise more particularly to him. We cannot ignore the attitude of contemporaries.

One series of incidents in connection with the conduit must be related here. In the days of the Restoration it was usual to honour the tradition that on days of public rejoicing the Conduits should run red with wine. Four occasions are recorded when this was done in Cambridge, at Charles II's coronation in 1661, and when King Charles II, King William III and Queen Anne successively visited the town, coming over from Newmarket in 1671, 1689 and 1705.[1] After that date nothing more is heard of the custom. We do not know how much water habitually gushed out from the Conduit, but clearly it would have needed a great deal of wine to make it run red for any length of time. Yet in 1689 the

[1] Cooper.

sum paid by the Mayor for making the Conduit run wine was only thirty shillings. Of the 1671 visit we are told that the Conduit ran with claret wine as the King passed by. Perhaps a momentary substitution of wine for water was accepted as a symbol in place of the more prolonged substitution which was then supposed to have been the custom in earlier generations.

CHAPTER VIII

THE WATER BROUGHT TO EMMANUEL
AND CHRIST'S COLLEGES

The third channel out of the conduit head leads to Emmanuel and Christ's Colleges and to St Andrew's Street. The construction of this channel can be dated with precision. It was under construction on 2 April 1631. This is known to us from a letter of that date written by Dr Joseph Mead. He writes:

Yet Dr Sancroft and Dr Chadderton getting me to walk yesterday with them to Spittlehouse end, and thence along to Balle's folly, to see the new ditch and workmen to convey part of the Whitehill water to Emmanuel Colledge and so downe by ours, I gott a cold with being too hot.[1]

The farm close to which the Nine Wells are situated is still called Whitehill. Ball's Folly was a large piece of waste ground on the east side of, and adjoining Hills Road, close to where the Perse School now stands.[2] Ball was the name of a former Town Clerk.[3] Dr Mead (1586–1638) was a distinguished biblical scholar, and a fellow of Christ's College. Dr Laurence Chaderton had been the first Master of

[1] *Christ's College*, by Peile, 1900, p. 139.
[2] C.A.S. "Cambridge Outside the Barnwell Gate", by Stokes, 1915.
[3] Cooper, 1574.

PLATE III

THE BATHING POOL

at Christ's College

Emmanuel, holding that office from 1584 to 1622. After his retirement he lived on in Cambridge until 1640, being more than a hundred years old at his death in that year. Dr William Sancroft (1582–1637) was Master of Emmanuel College from 1628 to 1637; he was the uncle of the better-known William Sancroft, who was also in his turn Master of Emmanuel College and who was subsequently Archbishop of Canterbury.

The story of the third channel is told by a recent Master of Christ's College as follows:

> In 1630 Dr Butts of Corpus V.C., collected a considerable sum to defray the expense and he gave £80 of this to carry a supply of water from the conduit house at the south end of Trumpington Street to Emmanuel and Christ's Colleges: to which colleges the right to this water was granted by the Commissioners of Sewers. The poor of the town were "set on work" to make this stream. It was recommended by the Commissioners that the colleges should allow a portion of the water to come into the street at Emmanuel Gate, and to run down the street so as to flush the King's Ditch at the end of it. The overflow still runs there, and into the sewer beyond Christ's Gateway. The "New River" as it was called, was to be cleansed by the two colleges from the conduit head downwards, and the wooden bridges over it were to be kept in repair. Of these there were several, one by the Almshouse, one near Parker's Piece, one by "the Maids' Causey"; also an "arched bridge" perhaps of brick, near Ball's Folly, already mentioned. The College accounts have frequent reference to this expense: for gravel required "to keep the new river from crossing the way", "scouring the new ditch", "clensing the

grate at parker's peece", etc. In 1638 the colleges contracted for £1. 10s. a year to have the river "clensed from Nunslake (probably a pond near Jesus College) to the end of our peece (Christ's Piece), to Emmanuel brewhouse (elsewhere described as Mr Entwhisle's) and from the turning of the water into Emmanuel through the bank and so along parker's peece and up to the Spittlehouse.[1]"

Dr Peile claims a share of Hobson's water for his college as a matter of right. The language of the Inclosure Acts is more cautious. In both the Inclosure Acts, for Barnwell (Little St Andrew's) 1807, and for Great Shelford 1835, provisos have been inserted to protect these two colleges, but the provisos purport to protect, not their rights, but merely their benefits and advantages.

Courts of Sewers were courts which were set up by the Crown as and when required in accordance with the Statute of Sewers of 1532 (23 Hen. VIII, cap. 5). They were temporary only and their jurisdiction was limited to the area expressly named in the commission. Their object was to regulate all water channels and embankments, for the word "sewer" was not then limited in meaning to those drains in which the water was foul. Several successive commissions appointed about this time included both the Vice-Chancellor and the Mayor as well as others, and these Commissioners held Courts and made Orders in respect of the great river, that is the Cam, as well as in respect of Hobson's New River. An order dated

[1] *Christ's College*, by Peile, 1900, p. 153.

23 April 1634, part of which is printed as Appendix IV to this book, decrees that the maintenance of the watercourse from the conduit head through Emmanuel and Christ's Colleges should be at the cost of the colleges concerned. Of recent years the two colleges have not themselves cleaned out and maintained this watercourse except within their own walls, but they have been accustomed to pay ten pounds a year to the Trustees of Hobson's Conduit and to leave the duty to that body

One of the bridges constructed in 1631 was known as Sentry Bridge, or alternatively as Stone Rake Bridge, but the reason for the names is unknown. This bridge was the one by which the traffic down Hills Road crossed the watercourse, just south of the four cross-roads now called Hyde Park Corner.

There is no record of the date of the construction of the bathing pool at Christ's College. The bathing pool at Emmanuel College certainly existed in 1688, for in Loggan's publication of that date it is shown both on the map and in the picture of the college. But the bathing pool at Christ's College is not shown by Loggan. The prominence amongst the busts around this pool of the funerary urn to Dr Mead may suggest that the pool was constructed before the fame of Dr Mead had evaporated, and Dr Mead died in 1638. Much later the pool is mentioned in a publication of 1763 named *Cantabrigia Depicta*.

An interesting sidelight is thrown on the construction of this branch of the watercourse by a passage in a textbook on surveying published, or perhaps reprinted, in 1662. The writer, George Atwell, mentions therein a certain

Mr Frost, then manciple of Emmanuel College in Cambridge, since sword-bearer to the Lord Mayor, and since that a secretary to the Counsel of State, a man beyond all exception for integrity of life, an excellent mathematician, one that brought the water from the Spittle House to Emmanuel, and thence to Christ's College.[1]

George Atwell died in the year 1658 aged eighty-two, and is buried in the chancel of North Runcton Church near King's Lynn. He is lauded on his gravestone as being "De Studio et Praxi Mathematiccis non Ignobilis". Mr Frost, although here acclaimed as being an excellent mathematician, was not a graduate member of the college. A manciple is an officer who buys provisions for an institution. The word mathematician seems to be used to carry the meaning which would now be conveyed by either of the words surveyor or engineer. Mr Frost's son Walter was admitted to the college in 1634.

[1] *The Faithful Surveyoure*, by George Atwell, 1662, p. 81.

PLATE IV

THOMAS HOBSON   *Portrait in the University Registry*

CHAPTER IX

THOMAS HOBSON, THE CARRIER

Thomas Hobson (1544–1631), during an exceptionally long working lifetime in the reigns of Queen Elizabeth and of James I, conducted a carrier's business between Cambridge and London. At that time much of the goods traffic was still by packhorse, but he is known to have possessed waggons with teams of horses in which he conveyed, not only goods, but also some passengers, women, children, and scholars, as we are told. He also kept riding horses which he let out to private travellers who hired them for the journey. Hobson was clearly something of a pioneer in the world of transport, and may be compared with the chairman of a motor omnibus company in our own day.

A great tradition collected round the personality of Hobson, a tradition connected with horses and with road travel. Successive generations of students spread fables about him over the whole country. The tradition began during his lifetime, for on his death Milton the poet thought it worth while to write epitaphs upon him, whereas he did not write epitaphs upon other Cambridge townsmen. John Milton of Christ's College (1608–74) was but twenty-two years of age, and not yet a Master of Arts, when Hobson died, and diverse opinions may be held about the propriety of the rather bantering tone of the epitaphs, but undoubtedly the subsequent fame of the poet helped to popularize the Hobson tradition. The tradition was firmly established within twenty-four years of his death, for Evelyn the diarist, writing of his visit to Cambridge in 1654 and mentioning Hobson's name, clearly assumes that the name will be familiar to his readers.

The traditional Hobson was shrewd, active, industrious, just and honest, a successful commercial man but an unpretentious one, and had a directness and even roughness of manner which was forgiven him and even enjoyed on account of his other qualities. The tradition is first presented to us in the verses beneath the early engraving[1] in which he is shown holding a bag of money. The verses run:

> Laugh not to see so plaine a Man in print,
> The shadow's homely, yet ther's something in't,
> Witnes the Bagg he wear's (though seeming poore)
> The fertile Mother of a thousand more:
> He was a thriveing Man, through lawfull Gaine,
> And wealthy grew by warrantable paine;
>> Then laugh at them that spend, not them that gather,
>> Like thriveing Sonnes of such a thrifty Father.

The Hobson tradition lasted until the railways drove horses and horse-drawn coaches off the roads. The substance of it as it was understood in 1802 is expressed in the letterpress attached to Kirby's engraved portrait of that date which reads:

Tobias Hobson, The Cambridge Carrier, and the first man who let out hackney horses, and from whom originated the famous adage, Hobson's Choice, that or none.

[1] Frontispiece.

And again:

Mr Hobson, the carrier of Cambridge, by the help of common prudence, and a constant attention to a few frugal maxims, raised a much greater fortune than a thousand men of genius and learning, educated in that university, ever acquired, or were even capable of acquiring.

The expression "Hobson's choice" is still current. As simply understood it means no choice at all. It arises from the story that customers who came to Hobson's stables to hire a horse were not allowed to choose that horse which they preferred, but were offered that horse and that horse only which was next in turn for work. It is said that in the form of "Hudson's choice" the expression was current as early as 1614, and it is suggested that it was therefore an adaptation when applied to Hobson of Cambridge, but however that may be, it is under Hobson's name that the expression became popular. Thus a plain seaman writes in his journal in 1661: "We had Hobson's choice, that or none."[1] Some eighty years after Hobson's death Steele and Addison considered that the expression "Hobson's choice" was worth an article in the *Spectator* (Appendix II), but Steele, with greater subtlety than a plain seaman, saw that the expression contained also this further implication, that even when there is plenty a man ought not to make such a choice as to hurt the next comer.

Hobson was born in or about 1544 and, as it seems

[1] *Barrow's Journal*, by Lubbock, 1934, p. 51.

probable, at Buntingford, in Hertfordshire, of which place his father was a native. The father, also called Thomas, was settled in Cambridge in 1561, in which year he was admitted by purchase to the freedom of the town, and at the time of his death in 1568 he was one of the treasurers of the Corporation. The elder Thomas Hobson was a carrier by trade, and the son succeeded to the business on his father's death.[1] Hobson, the son, lived at an inn called the "George", which, standing on ground now occupied by St Catharine's College, fronted on Trumpington Street.[2] The front part of the site of the "George" is now occupied by residential college buildings erected in 1930, and known as Hobson's Buildings, they adjoin the modern Bull Hotel. The back part of the site where presumably the horses were stabled is occupied by the college chapel erected in 1704. As his terminus in London Hobson used the Bull Inn in Bishopsgate. Hobson was never Mayor, but there is evidence that as early as 1604 he was regarded as a rich man. He held property in the villages of Cottenham, Chesterton and Waterbeach, all of which, however, seems to have been investment rather than residential property. His burial in the chancel of St Bene't's Church in Cambridge on 12 January 1630/1 is recorded in the parish registers, but there is no mural tablet nor tombstone to his memory. This church possesses a bible which Hobson gave them. The long tradition that he gave it is confirmed by an entry in it which is undated, but

[1] Cooper.
[2] Willis and Clark, vol. II, p. 78.

which is in the handwriting of the seventeenth century.

Hobson's sons died before their father, but he left behind him grandsons of his own name, and one of these in 1637 sold the George Inn to St Catharine's College. Hobson established one of his daughters, Elizabeth, with her husband, Thomas Parker, at Anglesey Abbey, Bottisham, some seven miles from Cambridge, and their descendants continued there for more than a century. The house is still an important residence. The name of Hobson's eldest daughter, Dorothy, may be read in the west of Cambridgeshire, in Guilden Morden Church, on a mortuary inscription which she erected there in memory of her first husband, W. Haye, Esq. This lady is buried at Salford Priors near Alcester, Warwickshire, where there is a life-sized effigy of her on her tomb in the church, and where also her name is mentioned on two mortuary inscriptions which she, being herself childless, erected to the memory of relatives of her second husband, Sir Simon Clarke. Her marriage with a baronet testifies to the very respectable position to which the family of Hobson attained.

In Cambridge the Hobson tradition was long preserved, though incorrectly, in connection with the White Swan Inn in Trumpington Street which, before it was pulled down in 1766, was known as Hobson's House. In truth the "White Swan" was the next house southwards of the former "George" where Hobson had lived, the "White Swan" being the northernmost house in St Botolph's parish. There was also a public house in Mill Lane called "The Old Hobson", which seems to have been pulled down or to have adopted a new sign in 1780. At the beginning of the last century Hobson's saddle and bridle were being preserved in the Guildhall as curiosities. There is now in Cambridge a street called Hobson Street, but it has no real connection with Thomas Hobson, the carrier. It came to be called after him in the course of the nineteenth century for the quite insufficient reason that it was then the headquarters of one or two firms of carriers of that later date.

The earliest engraved portrait of Thomas Hobson is that by John Payne (1607–47) who was old enough to have known Hobson personally. Payne represents Hobson on foot, upright, three-quarter length, and holding a bag of money. He has a lined weather-beaten face, and wears a wide-brimmed hat and a big cloak which are well designed to give protection to a traveller in bad weather. Both the Fitzwilliam Museum at Cambridge and the British Museum in London possess examples of Payne's engraving. Various other engravings of Hobson were published during the two hundred years after his death, but they are copied rather closely from Payne, like the one unsigned, belonging to St Bene't's Church, and like the one dated 1802 and signed R. S. Kirby, Paternoster Row, now in the Fitzwilliam Museum.

The National Portrait Gallery has a painted portrait of Hobson. This follows Payne to the extent of representing Hobson on foot, upright and three-quarter length, but in this painted portrait the weather-beaten old carrier of Payne's engraving has been transformed into a gentleman with a smooth face, a well-trimmed beard and a more fashionable hat, moreover a very genteel pair of gloves has replaced the bag of money. This portrait appears to be seventeenth-century work and to be posthumous. It may be surmised that this transformation of the carrier into a gentleman was an act of piety of some well-to-do descendant. John Bowtell the Cambridge antiquary, who died in 1813, tells us that there was formerly a picture of Hobson at Anglesey Abbey, and that Roger Gale had another supposed to have belonged to Mrs Katherine Pepys, who in her will dated 1700, bequeathed "Old Mr Hobson's picture".[1] In the new Cambridge Folk Museum there is, on paper of eighteenth-century date, a line and wash monochrome which seems to have been copied from the National Portrait Gallery portrait. It has been in the possession of the Town Council for some seventy years. It purports to have been at one time in the possession of Roger Gale (1672–1744), an antiquary who left his coins to the University Library and his manuscripts to Trinity College.

There are at Cambridge several painted portraits of Hobson. These owe but little to Payne's engraving. They represent Hobson, mounted, riding on a black horse. One of these hangs in the large room of the Cambridge Guildhall. On the back of it is the

---

[1] Cooper, vol. III, p. 236, quoting Bowtell.

inscription: "This picture was hung up at the Black Bull, Bishopsgate, London, upwards of a hundred years before it was given to J. Burleigh, 1787." The picture was bought in 1849 by public subscription from a Mr Swann, carrier and livery-stable keeper in Hobson Street, and the successor in business of Mr Alderman James Burleigh. Of this portrait we hear in 1840 that

> An original portrait of Hobson is to be seen at this hour at Mr Swann's waggon office in Hobson Street. He is mounted on a stately trotting black nag, himself bedecked in the finest possible garments. This portrait hung for a hundred years at the Bull, Bishopsgate Street, London, whence it was brought by alderman Burleigh, and left by him to Messrs Marsh and Swann who resisted the importunities of Dr Clarke to present it to the university library. It now ornaments Mr Swann's counting house.... Of the above-mentioned painting three copies were made by Freeman, and there are engravings of it.[1]

This alderman, James Burleigh, has left his name as that of a well-known street in Cambridge. He died in 1828 and was buried at St Andrew the Less at Barnwell. There was also an earlier James Burleigh who was Mayor in 1770 and died in 1786. The Burleighs were carriers, and ran to the "Black Bull" in Bishopsgate in London which is the same inn as that to which Hobson had been accustomed to run two hundred years earlier. James Burleigh, the younger, was an officer of the Patriotic Association of Cambridge Volunteers formed in 1798,[2] and a painted

---

[1] *Cambridge Portfolio*, by Smith, 1840, p. 312.
[2] Cooper.

portrait of him in the uniform of that corps is to be seen in the Folk Museum on Castle Hill.

There are two more painted portraits of Hobson, one in the Borough Library and one in the University Registry, which are very similar to one another and to the Guildhall portrait, except that Hobson is there riding in the opposite direction across the canvas. The portrait in the Registry was there as far back as 1856, but nothing more is known of its history. This portrait has recently been well restored, but those in the Guildhall and in the Borough Library are much darkened by age. There are also very similar portraits of Hobson on horseback, one in Cambridge in private ownership which has upon it the name of Freeman, and another at Thetford in the Guildhall.

There is yet another painted portrait at Queens' College, in the President's Lodge. At the foot of it there are some doggerel verses in English and Latin. It was given to the college unexpectedly a few years ago, and little or nothing is known of its history.

In the collection of coins in the Fitzwilliam Museum there are some token coins with an effigy of Hobson upon them. At the end of the eighteenth century it was for a time common for private traders to put into circulation their own token coins. Amongst others James Burleigh in 1799 issued token coins. His tokens represent, on the one side Thomas Hobson on horseback, and on the other the Conduit which then stood on Market Hill. The museum has three specimens, one is silver and two are copper; all three are from the one die which is by Hancock, die-sinker. All three have James Burleigh's name upon them, and round the rim of one of the two copper tokens are inscribed the words: "Value one Penny Payable at Cambridge."

The plaster bust of Hobson now in the Guildhall is modern. It is by a local sculptor named Henry Wiles. He is said to have followed an engraving published in 1795 by Calufield & Harding.[1]

The public spirit as well as the wealth of Thomas Hobson are shown by the foundation during his lifetime of a workhouse. It was founded for the charitable purpose of giving employment at wages to poor persons out of work, but a semi-penal department was attached to it to which stubborn rogues and beggars who refused to work could be committed. It was not a workhouse under the Poor Relief Act of 1601, it was a House of Correction under the Act of 1576, and like other Houses of Correction was frequently called a Bridewell, after the London House of Correction of that name. In our time the offer to an honest man of a day's work might be unacceptable if the work was to be done in the company of rogues and beggars, but there is no reason to impute such feelings to Hobson's contemporaries. This workhouse charity continued to attract other benefactions down to the time of John Bowtell who, dying in 1813, left £500 to the trustees of the workhouse for the apprenticing of poor boys. The fact that Hobson founded a workhouse for the setting to work of the

[1] *Cambridge Municipal Notes*, publd. Spalding.

unemployed rather than an almshouse for the aged or a school for the young, is in keeping with the virile character of the traditional Hobson. He himself worked continuously until he died at the age of eighty-six, and he expected others also to find happiness in work.

Hobson's workhouse stood on the site now occupied by the borough police station.[1] It was called the Spinning House, because in Hobson's day spinning was the task to which the unemployed could most conveniently be set. It is described in 1749 as being pleasantly situated near the fields at the south end of the parish of St Andrew,[2] and as the writer makes no comment on these buildings while condemning quite fiercely those of the gaol at the Guildhall, it may be assumed that these buildings were satisfactory by the standards of that time. A visitor in 1802 reports that to answer the founder's intention a woolcomber is appointed to the office of keeper, and he employs not only several hands under the foundation of the charity, but many others, among them his prisoners. This visitor thought the prison dirty, and found one prisoner only.[3] In its later years the building ceased to fulfill the founder's intention and was used solely as a place of confinement for women, and it was specially continued for this purpose after the date, 1865, when other bridewells were merged into our prison system. The

[1] C.A.S. *Proc.* vol. xv, "Cambridge Parish Workhouses", by Stokes.
[2] *Cambridgeshire*, 1753, by Carter.
[3] *Gentleman's Magazine*, 1804.

building was finally closed, and was demolished in 1901. The roof was used in the construction of a building in Station Road, Waterbeach, in which also some of the cell doors may be seen.

Towards the perpetual maintenance of the conduit Hobson bequeathed to certain trustees seven leys of pasture in Swinescroft. The Swinescroft, also called St Thomas' Leys, was situated between Pembroke Street and Lensfield Road. The word ley itself implies pasture land. These leys were lammas lands, that is to say, the owners enjoyed exclusive possession for a small part of the year only, the lands being thrown open for the remaining eight or nine months of the year to be grazed by the sheep and cattle of those who possessed lammas rights.[1] Hobson's Trustees held these leys for nearly two hundred years until 1801 when, in virtue of a private Act of Parliament of that year, they were purchased to form part of the original site and extensive grounds of Downing College. Nearly one hundred years later still the University bought the northern part of these grounds from the college, and the seven leys are now covered by museums and laboratories. Hobson's Trustees invested the purchase money which they received from Downing College in agricultural land at Over near St Ives, and after holding it for a century they sold it in June 1914 for £705 and invested in Government Stock.

Hobson also bequeathed a particular sum of ten

---

[1] *St Botolph's Parish*, by Goodman, p. 34.

pounds for the purpose of making the top of the conduit half a yard higher or more if it could conveniently be done. We have no record of what exactly was intended or of what was done. The word "conduit" in this context seems to mean the structure on Market Hill and not the watercourse along which the water travelled to it. The idea that half a yard has been added to the top of the Conduit as an addition to the original design and since its original construction must be dismissed, for the appearance of the Conduit as it now stands contradicts it. Perhaps Hobson's object was to raise the level of the lead cistern which the Conduit carried in order to facilitate the drawing of water. In that case it would have been necessary to raise the base of the structure, and this would have involved the demolition and rebuilding of the whole Conduit which would have been expensive. It is impossible to say whether anything of this sort was done.

CHAPTER X

OTHER BENEFACTORS OF THE CONDUIT

Thomas Chaplyn, gentleman, was Lord of the Manor of Trumpington in 1610. The source of the Vicar's Brook is in the parish of Great Shelford, and the conduit head is in the parish of St Andrew's, Barnwell, but nevertheless one and a half, out of the two and a half, miles between these two points lies across the manor and parish of Trumpington. It is probable that the straightening and deepening of the channel of the Vicar's Brook, by improving the drainage, increased rather than diminished the agricultural value of the land across which it passed, but even if Mr Chaplyn was advantaged by the undertaking, the whole tone of the deed of 1610 shows that he had been obliging in the affair. In return the University gave him the right to use the borough market, they gave to him and his heirs the liberty of purchasing in the market, and of carrying from thence sixteen quarters of horse corn annually for their necessary use.[1] The clerkship of the market had been granted to the University in 1561, establishing rights which were not finally extinguished until 1852. It has been quite common in England for markets to be under private rather than municipal control, and indeed there are some which are still so.

[1] Cooper.

The Town Council made Mr Chaplyn a freeman of the borough. Their book records his admission on "8 Jan 8 Jacobi 1610", that is 1611 in our new style, and the entry concludes with the words: "et juratus est pro toleratione Novi Rivuli et transitu in villa Cant."[1] In later years the following Lords of the Manor of Trumpington were admitted freemen of the town without fine in pursuance of the covenant in the deed of 1610: 1615, Thomas Gouldwell, gent.; 1623, John Barran of Trumpington, gent.; 1652, Richard Barran of Trumpington, gent.; and then in 1767, Thomas Clamtree of Colchester, Esq.[2] The Chaplyns continued in Trumpington for two or three generations after 1610, but were failing in 1693, for a record of legal proceedings of that date shows how the widow of the late William Chaplyn was then in serious financial difficulties.[3] It is not clear why the Lords of the Manor, being admitted freemen so recently as 1767, then ceased to be again admitted, whether the freedom ceased to be of much value, or whether it came to be considered that the deed of 1610 did not extend to those who derived from Mr Chaplyn by purchase. The dignity of the Lordship of the Manor has not yet been finally extinguished, and there is still a Lord of the Manor residing at Trumpington Hall.

The Cambridge New River was not financed out of the rates, for our system of rating was at that time

[1] Cole, Brit. Mus. Add. MSS. 5842, p. 370.
[2] Cooper.
[3] Cole, Brit. Mus. Add. MSS. 5842, p. 370.

aimed solely at the relief of the poor, having been but recently established by the Poor Relief Act of 1601. It was not financed by adventurers, that is by investors who looked for some return on their investment. It was constructed by the joint efforts of the University and Town. Fuller wrote in 1655 that the undertaking was effected partly at the cost of Dr James Montague, Master of Sidney Sussex College.[1] Sidney Sussex College was founded in 1596, and Dr Montague (1568–1618) was the first Master. He relinquished the mastership for the bishopric of Bath and Wells as early as 1608, but seems to have continued his interest in Cambridge. There is a portrait of him in his college hall, and his tomb is in Bath Abbey. Sidney Sussex College had this special reason for being a large subscriber, that the ditch passed through their college garden in the later, and presumably more offensive, part of its course. Cole, the diarist, seems to attribute the whole cost to Dr Montague who, he says, munificently at a cost of one hundred pounds brought clear running water into the King's Ditch.[2] But Cole wrote as late as 1748. Masters, who published his history of Corpus Christi College in 1753, tells us that some two years after the year 1604 Trumpington Ford was brought into the town, chiefly he apprehends at the expense of the University, his college then being a contributor towards it.[3] It may

[1] *Cambridge*, by Fuller, written 1655; ed. 1840, Prickett and Wright.   [2] Willis and Clark, vol. II, p. 739.
[3] *History of the College of Corpus Christi*, by R. Masters, 1753, p. 133.

PLATE V

THE TOMB OF DR STEPHEN PERSE *in the Chapel of Gonville and Caius College*

be observed that the special interest of Peterhouse, Corpus, and Pembroke Colleges was in that part of the King's Ditch which extended down Mill Lane, so that they may have been content with what had been done in 1610, and comparatively indifferent to the developments of 1614 and 1630. The antiquary Bowtell says that Christ's College contributed fifty pounds, but Bowtell wrote nearly two hundred years after the first construction of the conduit and he may perhaps have in his mind the extension of 1630 rather than the original construction of 1610.[1] No list has survived of the subscribers to the first cost of construction, but as the colleges were the largest and richest institutions in the town, we may accept Masters' belief that they contributed more money than the trading community.

Stephen Perse (1548–1615) was for forty years a fellow, and was for some time bursar, of Gonville and Caius College, and he was at the same time a practising physician. In the chapel of his college there is an imposing mural monument to his memory. Dying childless he left a large fortune to public objects. He founded fellowships and scholarships at his own college, and he founded the grammar school and almshouses which bear his name. These were formerly in Free School Lane and Pembroke Street, but are now in Hills Road and at Newnham. Further, he bequeathed eight pounds to the maintenance and repairing of the banks and current of the New River brought into Cambridge, to be paid

[1] C.A.S. vol. XLVII, 1915, p. 41, Stokes.

yearly for ever. The Master and the four senior fellows of the college were put in charge of all these funds. The charity is now administered, by the same trustees, in accordance with a Decree made by the Master of the Rolls in 1837, elaborated by Directions issued in 1841. By these orders the annual expenditure on Hobson's River has been increased from eight to sixteen pounds yearly. In his Will Dr Perse had asked that the work of repairing the banks should be entrusted to his servant Peter Thatcher so long as he should live, and it seems that in years gone by the Perse Trustees acted quite independently of the Trustees of Hobson and of Potto, sending a workman up the stream to clean it out or to repair its banks just as they themselves thought necessary. In recent years, however, the Perse Trustees have paid over the bequest annually to the Trustees of Hobson's Conduit.[1]

Edward Potto, a butcher by calling, was an alderman, and was twice Mayor, in 1602 and 1622. He was one of a committee of four appointed in 1614 by the Town Council to supervise the erection of the Conduit on Market Hill and the laying of the pipes thereto. He was buried in Great St Mary's Church in October 1632. By his Will, dated 7 Ch. I, it was April 4, 1631, he left two tenements situated in the parish of St Edward's in Cambridge in the Butchers' Row there, in order that the Conduit standing on the Market Hill in Cambridge, and the pipes belonging to the same, might with the profits be from thence

[1] Cooper, and *The Perse School*, by J. M. Gray. Bowes, 1921.

afterwards kept and maintained in good and sufficient repair. He directed that his loving friend North Harrison should, so long as he lived, receive and so use the rents. North Harrison was one of those who had sat with Edward Potto on the committee of the Town Council above mentioned.[1]

The two tenements were situated in Union Street, the street which connected Market Hill with Peas Hill. They were not contiguous; there was another tenement between them. They were on the east side of Union Street and opposite to the east end of St Edward's Church, against which other houses had been built, thus narrowing Union Street. In 1913 the Town Council bought these two houses from the trustees for £1500, and the first part of the new Guildhall which was erected in 1937 now covers their site.

The name Potto is now so rare that it has been assumed more than once to be a misprint for Potts. But the name Potto was formerly common in this neighbourhood. It may be read on a monument in the middle of the village of Houghton (Hunts) as one of the names of a gentleman who died as recently as 1871.

Joseph Merrill was a bookseller in Regent Walk, a street which ran directly towards the west door of Great St Mary's Church, occupying the ground which is now the Senate House Yard. Joseph was in partnership with his brother John. John Merrill

[1] Cooper, III, p. 63 note, Charity Commission Report, 1837, and *Mayors of Cambridge*, by A. B. Gray, 1922.

was Mayor in 1781. He was the fourth to be chosen for that office in that year, for three others who were chosen before him refused to serve. John Merrill, the Mayor, lived to be seventy-one years of age, and dying in 1801 was buried at Great St Mary's.[1] Joseph Merrill lived likewise to be seventy-one years of age, and died in 1805 at his house near the Senate House. He was possessed of very considerable property and, dying a bachelor, left a great number of legacies, to Storey's Charity, to Addenbrooke's Hospital, to the University Library, to the parochial poor, and so on, including two legacies to Hobson's Charity, for general uses £400, and for fencing and securing the watercourse £300.[2] This £700 legacy was at first invested, but when in 1842 the trustees were put to a heavy expense for replacing the old lead pipe from the conduit head to the Market Hill with a new iron pipe, they sold out capital, and considered that the capital of Merrill's bequest was extinguished. The Merrill's bookselling business was ultimately absorbed by Deighton.[3]

The endowments of Hobson and of Potto, now invested in trustee securities, together with the payment due from the Perse Trustees, today produce a little more than one hundred pounds yearly, and this generally suffices for the upkeep of the watercourse.

---

[1] *Mayors of Cambridge*, by A. B. Gray.
[2] *Cambridge Chronicle*, Oct. 19, 1805.
[3] "Cambridge Bookselling", Address by G. J. Gray, 1925.

PLATE VI

TOKEN COIN, *dated* 1799, *representing Hobson and the Conduit*

CHAPTER XI

THE CONSTITUTION OF THE TRUST

The construction of the Cambridge New River was due to the two corporate bodies, the University and the Town, but no new single corporate body was brought into existence for the purpose of owning and maintaining it. Nowadays a waterworks, including the pipe lines under the public roads, is considered to need an owner, and a limited liability company is commonly created for the purpose of owning as well as of managing it. But in its early days the Cambridge New River was not conceived as needing an owner. It was regarded like a river, like the Cam or the Ouse, which need regulation and protection but do not need an owner. It is true that, as regards Trumpington, the Lord of the Manor, by the deed of 1610, had leased for a thousand years to the University and Town jointly, all the soil of the new channel, ditch or watercourse which was parcel of his soil and was situate within the fields, waste and common grounds, but there was no similar acquisition of title in the other parishes through which the watercourse passed. Accordingly the New River was merely regulated by the Orders of the same Courts of Sewers as were set up in those days to regulate the Cam and other local watercourses. These Courts made Orders regulating the River Cam at least as far up as to the village of Abington and also made Orders regulating the New River. For instance, in 1627 a Court of Sewers made a variety of Orders for the preservation of the New River, and especially prohibiting the inhabitants of Shelford from destroying the banks thereof.[1] These Courts of Sewers made Orders on various persons, apparently riparian owners, to cleanse and repair the watercourse and to remove obstructions, and on some of the Cambridge parishes for money to pay the cost of repairs and maintenance; indeed, the Order of 1627 purports to establish something like a water rate over most of the southern parishes of the town. But the records give the impression that these Orders failed to achieve their object, and that Hobson's River was not properly cared for until, in addition to the work effected by the Perse Trustees, the endowments of Hobson and of Potto resulted in the establishment of a permanent body of trustees, whose sole object was the care of this water system, and who held some funds for the purpose.

When Hobson died in 1630/1 and left lands charged for the upkeep of the watercourse, he left them to three executors whom he named in his will. When Potto died in 1632 and left two houses charged for the same purpose, he similarly left them to three persons named in his will,[1] but they were not the same three persons. It appears from Potto's will that he intended that the oversight of the two houses and the use of the profits arising from them should ultimately be undertaken by the churchwardens of

[1] Cooper.

Great St Mary's, perhaps for the reason amongst others that these churchwardens had in 1535 been constituted a corporate body,[1] but there is no record that the parish officers of Great St Mary's were ever admitted to any share in the management.[2] It was clearly more convenient that the same persons should manage both the two bequests of Hobson and of Potto, and a deed of feoffment dated 1667 shows that such an amalgamation had by that date been effected. These feoffees, or trustees as we should call them, for the word feoffee became obsolete about a hundred years ago, were feoffees only of the endowments of Hobson and Potto; they were not feoffees of the watercourse and of the Conduit. But as the feoffees of Hobson's and Potto's bequests controlled most of the resources available for maintenance and repairs, they naturally came in practice to be the general managers of the water system. Their position was not very clearly defined. In the Inclosure Act of 1807 for the parish of Barnwell they are described, rather guardedly, as: "the person or persons who shall be empowered to superintend, direct, and manage, such channel or watercourse on behalf of the said residents and inhabitants", and very similar terms are used in the Inclosure Act of 1834 for the parish of Great Shelford. And writing to the feoffees on behalf of the University in 1842 the Vice-Chancellor of that date addresses them as: "The feoffees and other parties who have authority over Hobson's watercourse."

[1] Cooper.   [2] Charity Commission Report, 1837.

Until the year 1868 it was the practice that every twenty or thirty years the surviving feoffees transferred their property by deed to a new body of feoffees including both themselves and a number of younger men. Men of the best standing in the town served the office of feoffee, but very few, if any, members of the University so served.

The business of the Trust is now conducted, and the trustees are now appointed, in accordance with two Orders made by the Charity Commissioners in 1868 and in 1899. Previous to 1868 the feoffees, or trustees, held the capital of the endowment and received and used the income therefrom, but the legal ownership of the watercourse and its banks was not vested in them. Since 1868 both the capital of the endowment, and also the watercourse itself and its banks, have been vested in the Official Trustee of charitable funds, while the trustees continue to receive and use the income from the endowment for the maintenance of the watercourse and its banks.

The Order of 1868 was made at the request of the six feoffees then surviving: John Okes, Chairman, Charles Finch, Elliot Smith, George Salmon, Charles Salmon and Charles Orridge. The chairman, whose father had been a feoffee before him, was a retired Cambridge surgeon and was one of the original three hundred members of the Royal College of Surgeons founded in 1843. He was closely connected with the new Cambridge Waterworks Company, for the springs from which they took their first supply of water were on his residence at Cherry Hinton Hall.

This Order named ten local gentlemen and appointed them to be trustees for life in addition to the five already in office. These ten new trustees bore names most of which are still well known in Cambridge: E. Beales, ironmonger; G. E. Foster, banker; W. Eaden Lilley junior, draper; H. J. Matthew, grocer; G. W. Fitch, solicitor; J. Nutter, miller; C. S. Bulstrode, upholsterer; J. Odell Pain, draper; W. H. Hattersley, grocer; and Arthur Deck, chemist.

The Order of 1899 was made when the surviving life trustees began to be inconveniently few. This Order makes a more permanent arrangement than that of 1868. It provides that the Town Council shall appoint five trustees, and that there shall be also ten other trustees co-opted from time to time as vacancies occur. None of the trustees are now appointed for life, but for a term of years only. The new scheme was started off with the appointment by the Commissioners themselves of the first batch of ten co-opted trustees as follows: G. E. Foster, banker; W. H. Hattersley, gentleman; G. W. Fitch, solicitor; W. Eaden Lilley, draper; Arthur Deck, chemist; W. Kidman Bird, merchant; Hugh C. Foster, banker; S. M. Jonas, land agent; G. A. Matthew, solicitor; and J. Lilley Smith, Esquire.

The trustees while preserving their separate individuality now work in close touch with the Town Council. They hold their meetings in the Guildhall. They do indeed employ as their clerk a local solicitor other than the Town Clerk, but with the consent of the Town Council they employ the borough surveyor to maintain their watercourse and other property.

There was at one time some discussion, even some controversy, about the legal title of the Trust to the ownership of the watercourse, and as to how far their rights extended to the banks. The Orders of the Courts of Sewers need hardly be considered in this connection, for the conferring of rights of ownership was not one of their objects. The Inclosure Acts, however, are important. Now the watercourse from the Nine Wells to the conduit head runs through the three ancient parishes of Great Shelford, Trumpington and Barnwell St Andrew, for the ancient parish of Barnwell, now subdivided, extended round the south side of the borough so far that it included Brookside, the new Botanic Garden and Brooklands Avenue. All these three parishes have been "inclosed" since Hobson's day, that is to say, individual ownership of fields has been substituted for the former common field system of cultivation. This was done during or after the Napoleonic wars when an increase in agricultural efficiency and productivity was imperative. The inclosures of Great Shelford, Trumpington and Barnwell were effected by three Acts of Parliament dated respectively 1834, 1801, and 1807, implemented in each case by an Inclosure Award made a few years later by the local Commissioners appointed in the Act. These Acts and Awards give authoritative evidence concerning the ownership of the lands with which they deal. The two Inclosure Acts for Great Shelford and Barnwell include a proviso under which the jurisdiction of the Inclosure Commissioners is explicitly excluded not only from the watercourse but also from six feet of the soil next and immediately adjoining thereto on both sides thereof, the which were to be set apart for the exclusive purpose of conveying water to Cambridge. On the award maps for these two parishes, but not on that for Trumpington, the rights of the trustees along the banks of the watercourse are indicated by a dotted line. In the case of the Trumpington Inclosure Act, which is earlier than the other two, there is no explicit exclusion of Hobson's watercourse. Such an excluding clause was then regarded as superfluous, and indeed it was so, for the commissioners being aware that the soil of this part of the watercourse was held under the deed of 1610 refrained from dealing with it. Thus in the two parishes of Great Shelford and Barnwell the rights of the Trust, though not derived from, are confirmed and defined by, the Inclosure Acts, while in the parish of Trumpington the rights are derived from the deed of 1610, the validity of which the Inclosure Commissioners accepted without comment.

Nowadays, however, in respect of the whole length of the watercourse through the several parishes, it may be sufficient to regard the rights of the Trust as prescriptive, the title depending on, and being confirmed by, long continued and undisturbed possession.

It was too in connection with the Great Shelford Inclosure Act that the meadow at the Nine Wells was purchased.

CHAPTER XII

ROMAN AND MEDIEVAL WATERWORKS, AND THE NEW RIVER FROM WARE TO LONDON

The ancient Romans constructed artificial water-courses and brought water into their towns from great distances. In Italy and France great masonry aqueducts are the most characteristic of Roman ruins. In Britain, however, the towns were small, and the rainfall being adequate and perennial, wells did not run dry and great aqueducts were not needed. The Roman engineers were limited to a gravitational flow of water along an open channel or half-filled pipe, for the reasons that they had no powerful engine for the continuous raising of great quantities of water, and that their larger pipes were so unreliable under pressure that water could not be carried in a closed pipe down one side of a valley with the certainty that it would rise again in the pipe on the other side. Indeed, later engineers right down to the middle of the nineteenth century continued to be subject to these same limitations. In the thirteenth century our engineers were taking up the art of water supply at the point where it had been left by the Romans. At Chester, so early as the year 1285, a certain convent was supplied with water from a village named Christleton through a leaden pipe three miles long,[1]

[1] *Chester*, by Morris, 1895.

PLATE VII

THE OBELISK

at the Nine Wells

and it is known that most of the English abbeys had good water supplies.[1] In the library of Trinity College are preserved the plans of a piped water supply constructed in the twelfth century which brought water from three-quarters of a mile away to the conventual buildings of Canterbury Cathedral.[2] This plan follows the usual medieval arrangement with an accumulating cistern at the spring-head whence the water was led to a distributing cistern close to the centre of distribution. The plan contemplates that the distributing pipes should habitually withstand the pressure of a head of water of ten or twelve feet.

A number of medieval towns had their own artificial water supply, sometimes piped and sometimes led in an open channel, Hull, Bristol and Ipswich, amongst others. As early as 1250 a stream of water, still existing, was brought into the town of Tiverton from a couple of miles away.[3] Leading into medieval London there were a number of such artificial watercourses.[4] They led to a public cistern, to hold which an ornamental structure called a Conduit was erected, and from it the water was carried in pails to the house of the consumer.

In the sixteenth century many of the great towns were taking thought about their water supplies.

[1] *The English Abbey*, by Crossley, 1935.
[2] *Architectural History of Christchurch, Canterbury*, by Willis. London, 1869.
[3] *Tiverton*, by Dunsford, 1790.
[4] *Springs and Streams of London*, by Foord, 1910.

A few of them were able to take over systems which had belonged to dissolved monasteries. Of the new waterworks of this period one of the best known is the one which was constructed between 1587 and 1591 at Plymouth by the great Sir Francis Drake for the supply of the town and of the ships in the harbour. The surveyor whom Sir Francis employed to lay out the line of the new watercourse for him seems to have been a practical tin-miner. The springs are but seven miles from the town in a straight line, but the watercourse, or leat as it is called locally, adopted so meandering a course that it was twenty-four miles long.[1] This water system supplied a number of Conduits in the town from which the householders fetched water in pails, but in later years an increasing number of private houses were supplied by means of private pipe lines.

The famous New River from Ware to London is contemporary with the Cambridge New River. The first sod was turned at Ware in April 1609, and the water first flowed into the conduit head at Clerkenwell, where the offices of the Metropolitan Water Board now stand, at Michaelmas 1613. As early as 1571 the supply of London with water from northern Middlesex or Hertfordshire had been the subject of an Act of Parliament so that, previous to the simultaneous construction of the two New Rivers, there had been forty years of discussions which were also simultaneous. From the springhead near Ware to the conduit head at Clerkenwell it is twenty miles in a

[1] *Plymouth*, by Bracken, 1931; and Smiles' *Engineers*.

straight line, and the channel winding round the higher ground was, when first constructed, thirty-eight miles long; but although the London New River was a much greater undertaking than that at Cambridge the engineering problems involved were very similar. There were differences, however, in the objectives of the two undertakings, as well as in their financial organization. The objective at Cambridge was, at first, the flushing out of public ditches and sewers, whereas the objective in London was the supply of water to private houses for drinking and other domestic purposes. At Cambridge too the construction was financed by voluntary contributions, whereas in London certain adventurers, or investors as we should say, put their money into the undertaking hoping for some profitable return. As in the case of the Cambridge New River, so has the design of the London New River been attributed, but unnecessarily, to mathematicians whose names are known; not only to Edward Wright, but also to Thomas Bedwell. Bedwell, a senior contemporary of Edward Wright, entered Trinity College in 1562 and died in 1595. His works deal chiefly with the application of mathematics to civil and military engineering.[1] While the Trustees of Hobson's Conduit have never been accustomed to use any seal or coat of arms, the New River Company of London has used a seal the design on which shows the Hand of Providence, issuing from clouds, and distributing water over London, with the motto:

[1] *Mathematics at Cambridge*, by Rouse Ball, 1889.

"Et Plui Super Unam Civitatem", words taken from the prophet Amos (iv. 7). Cambridge people using the Ware road to London travel for a time along the bank of the New River after they have passed through Ware, and a very small divergence from the high road will bring them to the beautiful pond below the church at Amwell, one of the principal springheads of the system.

CHAPTER XIII

TECHNICAL SKILL IN
THE SEVENTEENTH CENTURY

In the library of Trinity College are preserved several scientific instruments which belonged to Sir Isaac Newton. These include a telescope to which a spirit-level is rigidly attached in such a way that the observer, by glancing at the level, can know when his line of sight along the telescope is truly horizontal. This instrument is inscribed: "J. Rowley fecit. 1703." Although the mounting may have been less convenient, this instrument is essentially the same as the Dumpie Level which is part of the equipment of every modern surveyor and enables him to sweep the horizon on a level line of sight. Hobson's River was constructed nearly a century before the days of Newton, and to Hobson's contemporaries the telescope, though recently invented, was not yet generally available, but instruments fitted with a backsight and a foresight like a modern rifle had been available from the earliest times and would have been quite accurate enough for laying out Hobson's River. Nor was the spirit-level, which is essentially a bubble in a curved tube, yet available for the purpose of giving an accurate horizontal line. For this purpose, as far back as Roman days, architects and surveyors had used a long trough of water, and the fact that water stood at the same level in each of the two branches of a U-tube had always been known.

Our modern spirit-level is so perfect that we can ascertain a horizontal as easily as a vertical line, but to Hobson's contemporaries the ascertainment of the horizontal was more difficult. As a rule the surveyors of that date ascertained the vertical from a plumb-line, and then deduced the horizontal by laying out a line at right angles to it. One device consisted of a metal isosceles triangle which was hung up, together with a plumb-line, from its apex, so that when the base was bisected by the plumb-line a line of sight along the base was horizontal. The astrolabe, which was the most important instrument to the medieval astronomers and surveyors, was very similar. It was a circular metal disk, marked round the circumference with angular measurements. It was suspended from a specified point on its circumference from a tripod or from the branch of a tree, and the surveyor could then be certain that one diameter across its face along which he could gaze was accurately horizontal. By Hobson's time the astrolabe was in course of being superseded by a primitive form of theodolite. This instrument is not suspended like the astrolabe, but is used upon a stand which is adjusted by means of a compass and a plumb-line.

But for an undertaking so simple as the Cambridge New River no levelling instrument so elaborate as an astrolabe, or a theodolite, or even a primitive theodolite, was necessary. A tolerably heavy capenter's square, consisting of two arms at right angles to one another, each, let us say, about 18 inches long, would have been sufficient, and such instruments were at one time in use. It would be suspended from its corner, and one arm would be adjusted to the vertical by means of a plumb-line, whereupon the other arm would necessarily give a horizontal line, and any small error in the inclination of the two arms to one another could be detected by repeating the observation after reversing the direction of the horizontal arm.

The ancient as well as the medieval engineers made their pipes of lead, but these lead pipes were not as a rule cast solid, or drawn, like modern pipes. The lead was cast in sheets which were then cut to the right width, and the strip so formed was then rolled into the cylindrical shape of a pipe, and the edges of the strip were soldered together. These seamed lead pipes could not stand very much internal water-pressure without developing leaks.

In the seventeenth and eighteenth centuries water pipes made of hollowed logs were much used in this country. Each log had one big end where the bore hole was big, and one small end with a small hole, and the small end of each log was thrust tight into the hole at the big end of the next log. Elm was preferred because it withstands the action of damp earth better than other trees. There is a natural limit to the bore of such pipes, a limit which does not obtain in the case of metal pipes; consequently it was often necessary to lay several of them alongside one another in order that a sufficient quantity of water might be conveyed. It was through wooden pipes like these that the water of the London New River was first laid on to private houses. These pipes too developed leaks under pressure, so much so that down to the first decade of the nineteenth century the London New River Company thought it wiser to refuse to deliver water at a higher level than the ground floor of the houses supplied by pipe line. A couple of old wooden water-pipes are preserved in the Cambridge Engineering Laboratory. It was not until the middle of the eighteenth century that iron pipes began to be used in connection with water-works.

PLATE VIII

COTTAGE ON HOBSON'S RIVER

near the Botanic Garden

CHAPTER XIV

CAMBRIDGE WATER SUPPLIES,
PAST AND PRESENT

In earlier days Cambridge people drew their water either from the river or from shallow wells. The old part of the town stands on a superficial layer of gravel overlying a thick layer of gault which is a nearly impermeable clay. Water can therefore be obtained from wells sunk to the bottom of the gravel some five to fifteen feet down. The larger houses would each have had a private well in their own backyard, the smaller would have shared a common well in the street. There is a private pump belonging to King's College still standing just inside their Clare Gate. One old public pump still stands on Peas Hill behind the Guildhall. There was formerly a pump just outside the south-west corner of Great St Mary's churchyard, and another in the north-east wall of Holy Trinity churchyard.[1] Previous to the great fire of 1849 there was, on what is now part of Market Hill, a street known alternatively as Warwick Street or as Pump Lane, and old pictures show the pump which gave Warwick Street this second name. No doubt the gravel soil did to some extent filter the water which was collected in these shallow wells, but with an increasing population and an increasing

[1] Hamond's map, 1574. *Cambridge*, by Le Keux, 1841.

pollution of the land-surface this amount of filtering became more and more inadequate. Our predecessors of that date did surmise that disease might be due to contaminated water, but they perceived it so dimly that long after the inauguration of the Cambridge Waterworks, eighty years ago, there were many people who still preferred the water from their own private well, provided it was reasonably bright and clear in appearance, to the water from the Company's pipes.

By the middle of the nineteenth century the progress of engineering had made it possible to bring into the town a greater supply of water, and also to distribute the water by means of reliable pipes to the various houses. But this was more than could be done in connection with the gravitational supply of Hobson's conduit, and a steam-pumped waterworks became necessary. In 1851 a Bill was introduced into the House of Commons for the incorporation of a Company which should supply the town with water from the Nine Wells, taking over also the rights of the Trustees of Hobson's Conduit. This Bill was, however, opposed, not only by the University and certain colleges, but also by the Improvement Act Commissioners for the Town, an *ad hoc* local authority for public health affairs which at that time existed in addition to the Town Council. The Bill was consequently withdrawn.[1] While it was generally agreed that Cambridge needed a new waterworks, complaint was made that this particular

[1] Cooper.

Company was being promoted by too small a group, and by persons who were not widely representative of the University and the Town. The group included an engineer from the Midlands and his friends, and a Cambridge solicitor with a few of his friends.[1] In July 1851 the *Cambridge Chronicle* hinted darkly that disclosures were to be expected in connection with this affair, but no disclosures seem to have come; political and religious partisanship were rather bitter in those days, and the solicitor in question and the *Chronicle* belonged to opposite parties.

The existing Cambridge University and Town Waterworks Company was incorporated in the year 1853. The Act of Incorporation includes a section especially protecting the rights of the Trustees of Hobson's Conduit. In 1855 the new waterworks were inaugurated by a public dinner at the Red Lion Hotel, the Rev. Dr Whewell, Master of Trinity College, and Chairman of the Company, presiding.[2] This Company's first source of supply was the group of springs at Cherry Hinton which arise from the foot of the chalk near the Robin Hood Inn and in the grounds of Cherry Hinton Hall. After a time these springs were found to be insufficient for the increasing needs of the town, and accordingly the Company supplemented this supply by sinking wells at Fulbourn and on the Cherry Hinton Road. These are to the north of the chalk upland and the ground here consists of a horizontal layer of gault clay from one to

[1] *Cambridge Chronicle.*   [2] Cooper.

two hundred feet thick, under which there is a layer
of greensand, under which again is a layer of
Kimmeridge clay. As the gault and the Kimmeridge
clay are impermeable to water while the greensand is
permeable, the greensand is full of the water which
fell as rain-water on the loose sandy beds of the
greensand outcrop some miles away on the boundaries
of Cambridgeshire and Bedfordshire. Some years
later it was urged that, as the gault was not perfectly
impermeable, a certain amount of surface water
might be penetrating through it and contaminating
the water below, and accordingly these wells were in
their turn abandoned, and the Waterworks Company,
reverting to the chalk, now supply the University
and Town from a well sunk directly into the chalk
farther south on Shardelowes Farm beyond Fulbourn
and near to the Fleam Dyke.

CHAPTER XV

THE MEDIEVAL WATER SUPPLY OF TRINITY COLLEGE

There is one system of water supply still in use in Cambridge which is older than Hobson's conduit. This now belongs to Trinity College. It brings water to the college from the neighbourhood of the Observatory.

The country west and north-west of Cambridge is composed of an impermeable gault clay upon which lie patches of gravel of no great depth. One such patch extends over the sites of the Observatory and of St Giles' Cemetery and on towards Girton, giving to the farm just west of the Observatory the name of Gravel Hill Farm. A good spring of water issues from this patch of gravel at a point some three hundred yards west of the Observatory and close to a modern house called "Conduit Head". The spot was known in the fourteenth century as Bradrusshe. In the year 1327 the Franciscans, commonly called the Grey Friars, laid down leaden pipes through which they brought the water of these springs into the town to their convent which stood where Sidney Sussex College now stands.[1] The old pipes were replaced in 1842 by new two-inch drawn leaden pipes, but subject to this the water system now in use is the same as that

[1] Willis and Clark, vol. II, p. 427.

which the Franciscans constructed. The distance
from the springs to the Great Gate of the college has
been measured as 2370 yards. The pipe passes under
the River Cam, and then under the library and the
dining hall and across the Great Court of the college.
To-day the principal function of the conduit is the
supply of the fountain in the middle of the Great
Court, but the pipe is tapped in the dining hall and
is used there and elsewhere within the college for
domestic purposes; moreover the water is led on to a
tap just outside the Great Gate of the college from
which the public have the privilege, or perhaps the
right, of drawing water. This privilege, or right,
whichever it may be, is now of little importance, but
previous to the establishment of the modern Cambridge Waterworks it was much valued by the
neighbours. That part of the original pipe line which
extended beyond the Great Gate and on to the site of
Sidney Sussex College has long since ceased to exist.
The street which is now known as Sidney Street was in
the sixteenth century called Conduit Street, from
which it may perhaps be inferred that at that date the
public were accustomed to draw water from a Conduit
which stood in that street fed from the pipe line of the
convent.

In the fifteenth century the King's Hall, the predecessor of Trinity College, was already exercising a
limited right to tap this conventual water-supply as
it passed close by their boundary and, after the
Dissolution, but before the foundation of Sidney
Sussex College, when the buildings of the Franciscan

Convent were more or less derelict, this water system was given to Henry VIII's reconstituted college of Trinity, and this college has used it ever since.

It might have been supposed that for the first half of the length of this watercourse an open channel would have been sufficient, and would have been cheaper to make and to repair, than a leaden pipe, but the documents which survive[1] imply that from the first the watercourse was piped for the whole of its length. The springs are nearly 50 feet above the level of the Great Court of Trinity College. At the present time the water gushes out of the fountain in the Great Court some 18 feet above the ground-level, so that where the pipes descend in order to pass under the river there must be a pressure of some 30 feet of water. It is permissible to wonder whether the seamed leaden pipes of the fourteenth century were sufficiently tight so that the water after falling below the level of the river would rise again in the pipes to supply tanks in the Conduits at the King's Hall and at the Grey Friars, or whether a hand-pump was necessary to lift it again from below ground. It is known that in 1434 the pipes needed frequent repair, for complaint was made in that year of the obstruction which was caused on the highway whenever it was necessary to dig up the road surface to effect the repair of the pipe below.

The Inclosure Act for St Giles's Parish is dated 1802, and in it there is a proviso for preserving to

[1] Willis and Clark, vol. II.

Trinity College their rights in this ancient water-course.

The Charter of King's College dated 1444 arranges for a water supply which was, however, never built, very similar to the Trinity conduit. The King's College Charter grants a piece of ground called "Holwelle" at Madingley, 30 feet square, belonging to Barnwell Priory, "near the grange called Morebernes belonging to the same convent. . . for the construction of a subterranean aqueduct to bring water to the college".[1] Moor Barns Farm, still so-called, is situated at the foot of Madingley Hill, on the main road to St Neots. It is at the extremity of St Giles's Parish, and the word moor is derived from the open pastures, or moor, of Madingley, beyond it. Moor Barns Farm is a mile farther from the town than Trinity conduit head, and a pipe from this farm would have run close alongside the Trinity conduit pipe, but the two sources are derived from different geological formations.

In the eighteenth century there was a bathing-place in a little wood two miles west of the town of Cambridge near the village of Madingley:[2] it was much frequented by Cantabs, the water being very good, and the walk thither very agreeable.[3] This bathing-place may well have been at Moor Barns. A century earlier, in 1653, Samuel Pepys and a

---

[1] Willis and Clark, vol. 1, p. 345.

[2] *Cantabrigia Depicta*, 1763, printed for T. and J. Merrill.

[3] *History of Cambridgeshire*, by Carter, 1753; ed. Upcott, 1819, p. 18.

number of his friends walked out from Cambridge to Aristotle's Well, where they slaked their thirst with great draughts of cold water from the conduit.[1] This might equally well refer to Moor Barns or to Trinity conduit head.

[1] *Pepys, The Man in the Making*, by Bryant, p. 23.

CHAPTER XVI

THE OLD ACCOUNT BOOKS OF THE TRUST

The recorded accounts of the trustees go back as far as the year 1710. The oldest book is long shaped, sixteen inches by six, and is parchment covered. The late Mr G. A. Matthew, formerly one of the trustees, examined these account books, and made some useful notes upon them. His manuscript, to which we are here indebted, is in the Borough Library.

The book begins with a list of names which are no doubt those of the feoffees in office in 1710. The list comprises: S. Urbin (?), W. Carter, William Stukes, George Frohock, W. Finch, A. Sumpter, W. Fuller, S. Lupton (or Lupson?) and C. Stukes. Of these we may suppose that George Frohock was a relative of that John Frohock who was Mayor in 1703. This W. Finch, ironmonger, was one of the trustees of the "Great Meeting", the predecessor of the modern Emmanuel Congregational Chapel, and he is buried in Great St Mary's Church where his gravestone may still be read on the floor just inside the west door.

The earlier accounts are entered, as Mr Matthew observes, in no very regular order. Pages and half-pages seem to have been left blank, and afterwards to have been used for accounts of a later date. Adam Sumpter was then acting as treasurer. The earlier pages purport to be accounts of "money received by

PLATE IX

BROOKSIDE

Trumpington Road

me Adam Sumpter one of the feoffees belonging to
the Conduit upon the Market Hill in the town of
Cambridge". They record payments made by the
various tenants of the leys, that is, meadows, which
had been bequeathed to the Trust by Hobson, and of
the houses which had been bequeathed by Potto.
There are payments for whitening the conduit and
for repairs. There are entries for refreshments at the
rent audit, but these are not excessive, certainly not in
the first half of the eighteenth century. The rents are
carefully collected, and are not permitted to fall un-
reasonably into arrear.

The old sign-post was sold for five shillings on
4 February 1723/4. It may be conjectured from
subsequent entries that this sign-post was a painting
of Hobson. Earlier, in 1712, we find: "paid by Mr
Randall for a new signboard of oak £1–10–10, Paid
Mr Wiseman painting the sign of Mr Hobson and
whiting the house £3–13–0," and again: "paid
carriage and receivage of his picture from Anglesey
Abbey to draw the sign by £0–5–0." The word house
here means the Conduit on Market Hill. At that
date Anglesey Abbey was still the home of the descendants of Mrs Parker, Hobson's daughter.

New feoffees appear in the books in 1731: John
Carrington, Richard Haseburn, Jeremiah Bosworth,
William Jardine, W. Wade, Robert Johnson and
Samuel Crossley, and a year later W. H. Finch,
Thomas Finch, William Jourdain and John Gibbon.
A new and useful practice was begun of appointing
two feoffees to act for the year, at the close of which

the accounts were to be laid before the whole body of
feoffees for examination, and two more appointed to
act for the coming year. William Jardine took a
prominent part for a long time, his name appears
frequently, becomes shaky, and in 1740 finally dis-
appears. A second William Finch acted as treasurer
for many years from 1734 onwards. He acts like a
banker, the feoffees sometimes pay him interest on
money which he has advanced to them. In August
1761 there is £13. 3s. due to William Finch, but by
July 1762 he is dead, and the £13. 3s. is due to
Madam Finch. This William Finch is comemmor-
ated on the east wall of the south aisle at Great St
Mary's Church.

New feoffees were appointed in 1750 in which
business Mr Thomas York was employed as attorney.
Mr York was Clerk of the Peace for the county, was
Mayor in 1738, and afterwards Town Clerk. He
lived in the house in Trinity Street now No. 34, and
is commemorated in St Michael's Church.

In 1752 the feoffees were Francis Hopkins,
Stephen Harrison, Charles Finch and Joseph
Ogrum, to whose number were added in 1753
William Chambers, and in 1755 Paul Godard. This
Charles Finch resided on Senate House Hill where
Caius College now stands,[1] died in 1787, and was
buried in St Michael's Church.

An entry occurs in 1762 to the effect that William
Chambers and Stephen Harrison take no interest for
money lent. There was a certain William Chambers

[1] Willis and Clark, vol. 1, p. 164.

who was twice Mayor in 1719 and 1734, but he died in 1747. The similarity of name suggests that this feoffee may be his son.

The feoffees in 1774 were King Whittred, Joshua Finch, Warren Adams, John Purchas, Richard Matthews and William Musgrave. Of these King Whittred was twice Mayor in 1762 and in 1772. He died in 1778 and was buried at St Edward's Church. He is said to have been an honest man who refused to succumb to the prevailing corruption.[1] Joshua Finch refused the mayoralty in 1781. His reasons are not recorded but probably the mayoralty involved more conformity than he cared to give, for the Finches were then Independents in religion. Several generations of the Purchas family served the office of Mayor. This John Purchas, also an Independent, was Mayor in 1771 and on his death in 1787 he was buried at Holy Trinity. In local politics, in which party feeling ran high at that time, he at first supported John Mortlock and the Rutland interest, but later on became estranged from them. Cole describes him as an oilman. It is claimed for the modern shop of Messrs W. Eaden Lilley and Co., Ltd., that they follow in direct line of descent from one of the Purchas family.

There is said to have been much mismanagement and even corruption in local public business during the fifty years which preceded the passing of the Municipal Corporations Act of 1835. In the case of Hobson's Conduit the payments on account of

[1] *Mayors of Cambridge*, by A. B. Gray.

refreshments after about 1781 do seem to become rather more frequent and considerable. We find £2. 14*s*. for expenses at the "Rose" when settling accounts, and £3. 9*s*. 8*d*. paid for dinner, etc. when the new feoffees were chosen, the "Rose" being the vanished inn on the Market Hill, whose yard has been continued as the modern Rose Crescent. The feoffees may have accepted the rather higher standard of refreshments which had become usual at this date, but broadly the business of this Trust was always quite honestly and efficiently administered. And indeed this is to be expected, for the motive of honesty was reinforced by the motive of self-interest, as most of the feoffees lived round the Market Hill and they and their wives used Hobson's water and were interested that it should be sufficient and pure.

In 1788 the feoffees were Thomas Markby, Thomas Smith, John Newling, James Burleigh, James Nutter, Thomas Verney Okes, another Charles Finch, W. Fisher and William Hollick. Of these John Newling, becoming an alderman in 1763, was then twice Mayor in 1774 and in 1776. His portrait still hangs in Addenbrooke's Hospital. He had been ousted from his mayoralty in 1775 on account of irregularities in his election in the previous year when party feeling had run very high over the question of King George III's dealings with the American Colonies. Thomas Verney Okes was for many years a surgeon in Trinity Street. He died in 1818 and is commemorated just inside the main door of St

Michael's Church. He was the father of the well-known Provost of King's College.

Amongst other notes at the end of the first account book is one to the effect that "the sign of Hobson is in old Carrington hands". Nothing is now known about this sign.

A new account book begins in 1788. In 1799 Charles Finch signs as treasurer, in succession apparently to his father, Alderman Joshua Finch, recently deceased. In 1805 James Burleigh presented to the feoffees two medals of Mr Hobson and of the Conduit, struck with a die, in his own possession. These have long since vanished out of the custody of the trustees; they were, no doubt, specimens of the private token coinage to which reference has already been made. In the same year, 1805, the seven hundred pounds bequeathed by Mr Merrill were invested in Government stock and a London banker was authorized to receive the interest.

The lighting of the Conduit at night began in 1806, in which year the feoffees paid £1. 12s. for lighting two lamps. Two years later the two lamps have increased to four. Gas is first mentioned in 1823 when £4. 18s. was paid to the Gas Company for lamps. The now existing Cambridge Gas Light Company was not incorporated until 1834, but the town was lit by gas as early as 1823, oil gas at first being used.[1]

Beginning in 1810 the feoffees developed the habit of subscribing quite considerable sums towards the

[1] *Cambridge Described and Illustrated,* by Atkinson and Clark, 1897, p. 231.

cost of making and maintaining public paths and roads, many of which had very little connection with the Conduit and watercourse. This was a very suitable way of using any surplus of income over expenditure. In 1810 fifty pounds was paid towards making a footpath from the conduit head house to St Andrew's parish, and five pounds was paid towards the paving of Sparrow Lane. In 1816 a subscription was given towards the making of a footpath from Hauxton to Trumpington. In 1816 £12. 11s. 3d. was paid for gravelling the path from Sentry Bridge to the conduit head house. In 1821 the feoffees subscribed £2. 2s. towards the widening of Sentry Bridge. This bridge was certainly inconveniently narrow in 1688,[1] but the road from Emmanuel College to the Gog Magog Hills had profited under the will of William Worts who, dying in 1709, had left £1500 for its improvement. In 1822 the feoffees subscribed £75 towards the iron bridge, that is, the bridge by which the roadway passes the Cam by Magdalene College, the structure of which, new in that year, is still in use. But meantime the watercourse itself was not neglected. In 1813 £12. 8s. was spent in cleaning the watercourse from Trumpington Inclosures to Spring Heads—186 poles at 1s. 4d. In 1821 the Nine Wells were cleaned out at a cost of £4. In 1826 John Webb, herdsman, of Shelford, agrees to keep the Nine Wells, and the brook in Shelford to the bounds of Trumpington, clean and in good order for £3 yearly.

For some years no mention is made of audit, but in

[1] Loggan's map.

1824 it is recorded that the custom was revived with an audit by John Purchas and Thomas Salmon. This is the John Purchas who was five times Mayor in the very last few years before the municipal reforms of 1835. All councillors and aldermen of that date were suspect by political reformers, so that it is of interest to observe that these feoffees, who were certainly honest, trusted John Purchas.

In 1836 the feoffees were G. W. Salmon, Charles Claydon and another Francis Hopkins. Charles Orridge, who joined them two years later, was a chemist whose shop on the Market Hill was one of those to be burnt out in the great fire of 1849. Under the title of Orridge and Sussum the business continued in another building on the Market Hill into living memory.

In 1831 a sum of £2. 2s. was paid to one J. Richardson, for a survey and plan of the pipe from the Conduit to conduit head. Probably the tracing now at Pembroke College is from this plan. In 1835 the feoffees spent £2. 2s. on fencing round the Close, that is, the three acres of land at the Nine Wells which was allotted to them under the Great Shelford Inclosure Act. In respect of the inclosure of the parish of Over the share of the feoffees towards the expenses of the Act and Award amounted to £20. 10s. 8d. which was paid in 1839. This figure is nearly two years' rent, and illustrates the magnitude of the legal expenditure involved in the making of these inclosures. In 1842 £1,116. 6s. 10d. was spent in replacing with cast-iron pipes the old leaden pipes which carried the water from the conduit head to the Market Hill. In 1850 the unusually large sum of £141. 7s. 11d. was spent on the repair of the banks. The sum of £25. 14s. 10d. was paid in 1856 to Swann Hurrell for iron fencing at the conduit head house. This is presumably the fencing which is still to be seen there. And in 1860 a further sum of £13. 10s. was paid to Swann Hurrell for iron.

Various subscriptions are paid: in 1856 £20 to the fund for the re-erection of the old Conduit, in 1861 £20 towards the obelisk in memory of Hobson, meaning no doubt the obelisk at the Nine Wells, and in 1865 £10 towards the improvement of Lensfield Road. Moneys were received from the Perse Trustees. In 1869 the Rev. J. Lamb, bursar of Gonville and Caius College, paid a contribution of £60 on behalf of the Perse Trustees towards fencing and repairs to the banks. In 1876 a sum of £25 was received from them towards the repairs of the banks, and in 1891 a further sum of £20. In 1887 Hobson's Trustees received a subscription of £10 from the Walpole Trust at Trinity Hall. The Walpole Trust held an endowment which had been bequeathed by the Elizabethan Dr Mowse and others of this college for the upkeep of highways, particularly the road to Ware. In 1886 a sum of £18. 9s. 6d. was paid to Mr G. J. Smith, surveyor of Green Street, for his excellent report and plans. These are still in the hands of the Trustees.

In these latter days Hobson's Trust continued as in earlier days to command the services of the leading

men in the town. In 1871 the accounts are signed by
Mr Henry John Matthew. This gentleman died in
1879. In 1880 Mr William Eaden Lilley signed, and
in 1899 Mr George Kett, who was several times
Mayor. In the following year, 1900, the signatories
are Messrs John Lilley Smith, William Kidman
Bird and Algernon Sidney Campkin, names which
bring the story down to our own times.

CHAPTER XVII

THE MORE RECENT HISTORY
OF THE CONDUIT

Of the ancient King's Ditch little now remains. As far back as 1753 it had already ceased to be more than a curiosity of antiquarian interest, for a description of the town of that date, after relating the history of the Ditch, goes on:

and the remains of it is that small ditch which passes through Pembroke Lane, Holiday's Garden, by Hog Hill, the back gate of the Falcon Inn, near the west end of St Andrew's Church, through Walls Lane, Sidney Close, Jesus Lane, and then through Jesus Green into the river.[1]

Presumably Holiday's Garden was the garden which soon after that date became the first University Botanic Garden. The dates at which the various sections of the open military moat of the King's Ditch were first converted into covered drains and later disused are unrecorded. Across the garden of Sidney Sussex College the Ditch, shown uncovered in Loggan's map of 1688, is covered over in the maps of 1798 and 1801. The portion in Walls Lane had been covered in before 1688. In some parts of Hobson Street and across the garden of Sidney Sussex College the brick-arched underground drain, some four feet high, still exists, but it has long been disused. In

[1] *History of Cambridgeshire*, by Carter, 1753; ed. Upcott, 1819, p. 14.

Hobson Street it is full of earth for three-quarters of its height. The line of the Ditch across Sidney Sussex College garden is still obvious enough, but elsewhere the only surviving vestige of the Ditch is the alignment of certain streets, St Tibb's Row and Park Street.

As the Ditch progessively became filled up, so progressively the flushing of it by the water of Hobson's River ceased. A tracing in the archives of Pembroke College dated 1832 shows how at that date some water was still being conducted round the back of the college into the pond in the old Botanic Garden. The water was led into the pond whence the overflow ran under the site of the modern Masonic Hall and into a short surviving piece of the Ditch in St Tibb's Row labelled the Black Ditch. Further, in a letter to the feoffees of the conduit dated 1842, soon after the laying out of the new Botanic Garden, the Vice-Chancellor, asking for a supply of water for the pond in the new Garden, reinforces his request with the reminder that up to that date the Frog Pond in the old Garden had been filled from Hobson's River. In the second half of last century the area of the old Botanic Garden became covered with museums and laboratories; it was then that Hobson's water issuing from behind Pembroke College was switched off into the public drain in Pembroke Street, and it was then that the last traces of the King's Ditch above ground vanished.

But, long after the flushing of the King's Ditch had ceased to be of much importance, the fountain of pure drinking water on Market Hill continued to be appreciated. That appreciation is expressed by Carter in 1753 in his *History of Cambridgeshire*. After writing about the Guildhall, he goes on:

Fronting the north side of the said hall stands a grand and very useful Conduit, built A.D. 1614 by Thomas Hobson, a carrier (who was buried January 12th 1630 in Bennet chancel), which has three spouts that continue running day and night. The water which feeds it is conveyed thither in a leaden tube which is laid in the earth for more than half a mile. The said Hobson not only erected it as aforesaid, but left the rent of seven lays of pasture ground in St Thomas' lays to keep the same in repair. And Edward Potto, alderman of the town, gave two tenements in Butcher-Row for the same use. And by carrying water from this Conduit to several parts of the town many poor people get a tolerable living.[1]

Similar appreciation is expressed in various other books, amongst others in Nicholson's *Guide to Cambridge*, published in 1804, in which it is stated that

the Conduit was erected in 1614 at the charge of Thomas Hobson, the celebrated carrier. It is built of stone decorated with rude carvings, and enclosed with an iron palisade. The water which is conveyed by an underground aqueduct to the Conduit continues always running through four spouts supplying the neighbourhood with a never failing stream of excellent water.

The fact that Merrill left money to the Conduit in 1805 shows that at that date it was still regarded as

[1] *History of Cambridgeshire*, by Carter, 1753; ed. Upcott, 1819, p. 18.

being of great importance to the town. Not only was Merrill a leading man in the town, but also he lived near Great St Mary's and, no doubt, he and his household used the water from the Conduit.

So late as 1856, the year after the inauguration of the modern waterworks, the Town Council considered the Conduit to be still so important that in that year they made Official Bye-laws prohibiting the fouling of Hobson's River.

The delivery of water into private houses by means of a system of pipe lines was never undertaken in connection with Hobson's New River at Cambridge as it was undertaken by the New River Company of London. Perhaps the quantity of water available was thought to be insufficient for this purpose. It was for any citizen who cared to do so to go to the Conduit with his pail and fetch away such water as he needed, and indeed any citizen may still do so. When in 1788 there was a local Bill before Parliament for the better paving, cleansing and lighting of the town of Cambridge, both the University and the Town petitioned that provision might be made in the Bill for supplying the inhabitants of the University and Town with water from the public conduit called Hobson's Conduit.[1]

In the last few years of the eighteenth century the watercourse in Trumpington Street from Addenbrooke's Hospital to Pembroke College gateway was completely reorganized. Until that date the water had flowed down the street in a single channel.[2]

[1] Cooper. [2] Fuller's map, 1634; Loggan's map, 1688.

Mr Gunning, M.A., Esquire Bedell, in his reminis-
cences published after his death in 1854, gives an
account of the inconvenience and accidents which
followed from the former arrangement. Discussing
the need which existed in 1794 for the better paving
and lighting of the town, he writes:

> Along the whole front of Pembroke College was a water-
> course which divided the street into two very unequal parts,
> the west side was by necessity the carriage road, but was only
> one-third the width of the road which adjoined the college
> and was appropriated for foot-passengers. The sides of the
> channel were boarded, and it was crossed by two very narrow
> bridges, one opposite the Master's Lodge and the other
> opposite the gates of the college.
>
> The principal inn at that time was the Cardinal's Cap,
> situated in the middle of the space now occupied by the Pitt
> Press. It happened not unfrequently that gentlemen's coach-
> men who were strangers to the town mistook the road between
> the college and the watercourse for the carriage way road, in
> consequence of which there was often much confusion, and
> occasionally accidents occurred.[1]

It is recorded in the books of Pembroke College
that in 1789 it was agreed that the town should
widen Trumpington Street by taking in a strip of the
street frontage to which the college had a claim, from
which it appears that even before 1794 the condition
of the street had been receiving the attention of the
authorities. The date at which the two runnels which
exist to-day were substituted for the single channel

[1] Gunning, vol. 1, p. 319.

was certainly earlier than 1815, which is the date of Ackermann's engraving of Pembroke College. In Custance's map, which is dated 1798, neither the single channel nor the two runnels can be clearly distinguished, but as the single channel was an important surface feature, far more so than the two runnels, the omission of the single channel suggests that it had been removed. Altogether it may be supposed that the change was made very soon after 1794.

In 1835 the University and Town acquired, jointly, the freehold of three acres of land immediately surrounding and contiguous to the Nine Wells. The occasion for this transaction was the inclosure of the common fields of Great Shelford following the Inclosure Act of 1834. In the Award which follows the Act the land is described as lying in the Back Moor, Sheep Common and Baillies. The Award fixes £126 as the price to be paid by the purchasers, which sum would go to those who had possessed common rights. In fact the University gave £150 and the Town gave £50, making a total of £200, for this allotment of common. The legal and other expenses were therefore considerable. At that date, however, the importance of the water supply was such that the land was well worth the money which was expended in acquiring it.

Writing in 1845, Cooper complains that the inscription on the Conduit, stating it to have been erected at the sole charge of Thomas Hobson, the celebrated carrier, is certainly incorrect.[1] It is to the adjective

[1] Cooper, vol. III, p. 62 note.

"sole" that Cooper with justice objects. This inscription is not carved in stone but is painted on the plaster of the structure and is repainted from time to time, and it has long since been altered so that it is not now open to Cooper's objection.

The inscription to which Cooper objected began with the words: "Thomas Hobson, late Carrier between London and this Town, in his Life-time, was at the sole charge of erecting this structure." This was on the north side of the Conduit. Another inscription on the south side commemorated Edward Potto.[1]

In 1842 the old leaden pipes from the conduit head to the Conduit on Market Hill were replaced by cast-iron pipes. These are for the greater part of their length still in use, but a short section was relaid in 1896. This was the section which had led across the paddock of Downing College, an area which at that time had recently been sold by the college to the University and was about to be utilized for the erection of museums and laboratories.

In 1849 there was a great fire which destroyed a number of old houses which had stood, backing on Great St Mary's Church, on part of the site of the present Market Hill. The opportunity was taken to enlarge the Market Hill and the old houses were not rebuilt. It was in connection with this development that the new fountain was erected in the centre of the Market Hill, and that the old fountain, called

[1] *A Concise and Accurate Description of the University, Town, and County of Cambridge*, printed 1790, for T. and J. Merrill.

Hobson's Conduit, was removed and re-erected at Lensfield Corner. On the old L-shaped Market Hill the old Conduit stood near the opening into Petty Cury. Its appearance there is recorded for us in several pictures: in a print of Rowlandson's of 1801, a copy of which may be seen hung up in the Borough Library; in the *Cambridge Portfolio*, edited by Smith, 1840; and in an engraving which is to be found in the *Memorials of Cambridge*, by Le Keux, 1841 and later editions.

Quite a bitter quarrel raged in the town in 1851 and 1852 as to whether there was or was not a right-of-way for the general public along the banks of Hobson's River across the parish of Trumpington, or alternatively whether the Trustees could give permission to the public to walk up and down the banks there. The quarrel centred on that part of the watercourse which extends from Finch's Walk to the Long Road: it seems that those who were interested in the Walk were desirous of continuing it into the parish of Trumpington. The farm on either side of this part of the watercourse then belonged to Trinity College, but was leased by that society to F. C. J. Pemberton, Esq. The farmer, who occupied under Mr Pemberton, erected a barrier across the western bank at the point where the parish of Trumpington joined the ancient, and then existing, borough boundary.[1] The barrier is a formidable iron gateway furnished with iron spikes. It still stands, though happily now open. Apparently the standing

[1] Cooper.

political and religious parties of that time took sides.
The conservative newspaper admits that a new footpath would be pleasant, but takes the opportunity to
observe how radicals show their inherent tyranny of
disposition and their desire to ride roughshod over a
college or a protectionist.[1] The word "protectionist"
refers to the Corn Laws which had been repealed so
recently as 1846. In its purely legal aspect the dis-
pute was held to depend on the exact terms of the
deed of 1610 which undoubtedly went so far as to
give to the Trustees themselves and to their agents the
right to walk along the banks of the watercourse for
the purpose of cleaning it. The University who, with
the Town Council, were the joint lessees of the watercourse, pointed out that the original lessor, Mr
Chaplyn, granted the lease from a generous motive
without valuable consideration in furtherance of a
particular benevolent purpose, that of maintaining a
watercourse, not of creating a right-of-way, so that
any attempt to establish by a technical and legal
construction of the deed rights not necessary to the
main purpose of the lease would be unseemly.[2] This
view was in effect accepted and no further steps were
taken.

In our own day, in connection with a modern town-
planning scheme, the proposal for a public footpath
the whole way up Hobson's River to the Nine Wells
and out on to the road beyond has been revived. This
will, however, be subject to some arrangement be-

[1] *Cambridge Chronicle,* 10 Jan. 1852.
[2] *Cambridge Chronicle,* 6 March 1852.

tween the public authorities on the one hand and the adjacent landowners and the Trustees on the other.

Peterhouse, like its neighbour Pembroke College, made use of the water of Hobson's river. A grating is still to be seen under the western of the two runnels in Trumpington Street from which a feed pipe, passing underneath the new Courtauld Gallery of the Fitz-william Museum, leads into the Peterhouse grounds behind. It is known that in 1748 and for sixty years thereafter there was a bath in the fellows' garden.[1]

The last considerable change was the abandon-ment some thirty years ago of that part of the original open channel which extended from the conduit head to Addenbrooke's Hospital. This part of the original ditch did not, like the lower part from Addenbrooke's Hospital to Pembroke College, run down Trumping-ton Street, but, passing between No. 1 Lensfield Road and No. 1 Trumpington Street, it flowed behind the Trumpington Street houses, Nos. 1–22, as far as the Hospital. In some places, notably behind Nos. 2 and 18, the channel may still be seen, dry and partly filled in. The line of the old channel still has this much importance that it is the boundary line between separate properties, for while the houses here fronting on the street are separate freeholds, some of the gardens behind them, being on the other side of the old ditch, belong to another owner, until recently to Corpus Christi College, but now to the Hospital. The plan dated 1832 shows the old open ditch still in use leading the water into the south end

[1] Willis and Clark, vol. III, p. 589.

of Addenbrooke's Hospital moat. Out of the north
end of the moat at that date three pipes emerged, two
leading one to each of the two street runnels, and the
third leading on under the sidewalk of the street down
to Pembroke College Chapel and then round behind
that college and into the old Botanic Garden. The
plan of 1832 also shows how the Trumpington Street
runnels then welled up opposite the north end of
Addenbrooke's Hospital front, being thus shorter
than they now are by some fifty paces. The later plan
dated 1886 shows how the pipe laid under the side-
walk of the street and leading to the old Botanic
Garden was still fed from the hospital moat and so
from the old open ditch behind the houses, but it
shows how at that date the two street runnels were
already, as at present, welling up opposite to No. 6
Trumpington Street and were being fed by a pipe
direct from the conduit head quite independently of
the old open ditch. There was also for many years yet
another pipe which led from the conduit head to the
laundry of Addenbrooke's Hospital, which until 1912
used this water.

The importance of Hobson's Conduit to the town
has faded since the inauguration eighty years ago of
the modern steam-pumped waterworks which now
supplies nearly all the drinking water needed in the
town; and the modern practice and art of street
cleaning is so thorough that for that purpose the
runnels in Trumpington Street and St Andrew's
Street are no longer of any great practical importance.
But in the history of public water supplies Cambridge

is remarkable amongst other towns in that it has still in operation two ancient systems, both the Trinity College conduit dating from the fourteenth and Hobson's Conduit dating from the seventeenth century.

But as the River Cam, chiefly because it has ceased to be used as a commercial highway for barges, has become with the gardens on its banks one of the outstanding beauties of the town, so also Hobson's New River, though no longer of much practical importance for water supply or sanitation, continues to be a source of enjoyment to all those who appreciate the history and the beauty of Cambridge.

APPENDIX I

Two *Epitaphs* on T H O M A S H O B S O N, *Carrier*
of *Trumpington Street*

The former is one of two not dissimilar epitaphs
written by the poet Milton when he was quite a
young man at Christ's College. The latter, typical of
the Hobson tradition, is from the manuscript remains
of the eighteenth-century Cambridge diarist, the Rev.
William Cole, who relates how a friend of his found
the verses amongst the papers of a Cheshire squire
recently deceased.

I

On T H E U N I V E R S I T Y *Carrier*

who *sickened* in the *time of his vacancy*, being *forbid*
to go to *London* by *reason* of the *plague*

Here lies old Hobson. Death hath broke his girt,
And here, alas! hath laid him in the dirt:
Or else, the ways being foul, twenty to one,
He's here stuck in a slough, and overthrown.
'Twas such a shifter that, if truth were known,
Death was half glad when he had got him down:
For he had any time this ten years full
Dodged with him betwixt Cambridge and the Bull.

And surely death could never have prevailed,
Had not his weekly course of carriage failed:
But lately, finding him so long at home,
And thinking now his journey's end was come,
And that he had ta'en up his latest inn,
In the kind office of a chamberlin
Showed him his room where he must lodge that night,
Pulled off his boots, and took away the light.
If any ask for him, it shall be said,
"Hobson has supped, and's newly gone to bed".

II

An A n o n y m o u s *Epitaph*

Here lies Hobson amongst his many betters
A man unlearned yet of *many letters.*
The schollers well can testify as much
But he received them in his pregnant *pouch.*
His *carriage* is well-known: oft hath he gone
An embassy betwixt father and a son.
In *Cambridge* few, in good time be it spoken,
But will remember him by some good *token.*
From hence to London rode he day by day
Till death benighting him he lost his way.
No wonder is it that he thus is gone
Since most men know he long was *drawing on.*
His team was of the best, nor could he have
Been *mired* in any ground, but in his grave,
And here he sticks indeed, still like to stand
Until some angel lend his helping hand.
So rest in peace: thou ever toiling swain
And supreme waggoner: next to *Charles's Wayn.*

APPENDIX II

The *Spectator* was a daily newspaper written by Joseph Addison and Richard Steele and issued in the days of Queen Anne from March 1711 to December 1712. Number 509, issued on 14 October 1712, contains an essay on Frugality written by Richard Steele. It is in the form of a letter written by Mr Hezekiah Thrifty to Mr William Spectator. Steele and Addison were both educated at Oxford, which may account for their carelessness in the matter of a Cambridge carrier's Christian name. The last quarter of the essay is as follows:

I shall conclude this discourse with an explanation of a proverb, which by vulgar error is taken and used when a man is reduced to an extremity, whereas the propriety of the maxim is to use it when you would say there is plenty, but you must make such a choice as not to hurt another who is to come after you.

Mr Tobias Hobson, from whom we have the expression, was a very honourable man, for I shall ever call the man so who gets an estate honestly. Mr Tobias Hobson was a carrier: and being a man of great abilities and invention, and one who saw where there might good profit arise, though the duller men overlooked it, this ingenious man was the first in this island who let out hackney horses. He lived in Cambridge: and observing that the scholars rid hard, his manner was to keep a large stable of horses, with boots, bridles, and whips, to furnish the gentlemen at once, without going from college to college to borrow, as they have done since the death of this worthy man. I say, Mr Hobson kept a stable of forty good cattle, always ready and fit for travelling: but when a man came for a horse, he was led into the stable, where there was great choice, but he obliged him to take the horse which stood next to the stable door: so that every customer was alike well served according to his chance, and every horse ridden with the same justice: from whence it became a proverb, when what ought to be your election was forced upon you to say " Hobson's choice". This memorable man stands drawn in fresco at an inn (which he used) in Bishopsgate Street, with an hundred pound bag under his arm, with this inscription on the said bag: "The fruitful mother of a hundred more." Whatever trades-man will try the experiment, and will begin the day after you publish this my discourse to treat his customers all alike, and all reasonably and honestly, I will ensure him the same success.

APPENDIX III

Copy of a *Letter* from DR ANDREW PERNE,
Vice-chancellor of the University

TO LORD BURGHLEY, *the Chancellor*,

Dated from Cambridge on January 18th 1574/5

The original is in the Record Office in London, and is indexed, State Papers, Domestic, Queen Elizabeth, 12, vol. 103, No. 3, 1575.

This letter is printed here at length because it has not previously been published. It should be read in connection with Dr Perne's letter to Lord Burghley of 21 November 1574 which is printed at length in Cooper's *Annals*, and is summarized in Chapter IV of this book.

Dr Perne's spelling and punctuation have here been modernized. He writes:

My duty in most humble wise remembered unto your honour: This shall be to certify the same that the university is returned again to their accustomed exercises of learning in the schools at the beginning of this term, which was the 14th of this January, saving the scholars of St John's and of Christ's College, the which continue in their exercises, those at Hilton[1] and the other at *(illegible)*,[2] the which I wish should remain there still, until the town be more clear of the plague.

[1] Hilton in Hunts., Baker's *History of St John's College*, ed. Mayor, p. 445.

[2] Probably Malton near Shepreth, *Christ's College*, by Peile, 1900, p. 37.

For the which we have taken the best order that we can to keep the sick from the whole. And yet the poorer sort, for the great desire that they have to enjoy the continuance of the relief that is charitably made for such households as be visited or that dwelleth near unto them that they should not go abroad, they do wickedly labour so much as they can by going abroad in the night time to continue the plague. Wherefore we think it good to put all those that be poor, that are or shall be, sick, into one place where they shall have all things necessary, out of the which they shall not go until it shall be thought convenient. All the colleges, thanks be to God, are hitherto free from the plague. There hath died in the town of the plague since my last certificate, which was the 16th of December, until this day, eleven in Trinity parish only. I trust in God that this frost will purify the whole, and consume the infection. And I trust the worst is passed, or else we shall be compelled to break up again, the which will be a great decay and hindering of learning in the university and the utter undoing of the town, whereof I would be right sorry.

I have according to your honour's commandment provided a workman from Lynn for the taking of the level of the ground at Trumpington Ford to convey that water into the King's Ditch for the scouring of the same, whose advice and judgement I do send to your honour here enclosed. There is one other in Cambridge who hath taken a level from the mills in Cambridge, to convey that water into the said King's Ditch, the which being nearer adjoining together, may (*illegible*) lesser charge. Whose judgement I likewise send unto your honour, most humbly craving your lordship's advice therein.

I have in most earnest wise, and often times, called upon Mr Mayor and others that hath (*part?*) chargeable with the scouring of the said King's Ditch, that they should now in this time of winter and frost set upon the scouring of the said ditch, and also for the renewing of an old composition betwixt the university and the town for the clean and wholesome keeping of the streets, the neglecting whereof in times past hath been a great occasion of this present infection to the great hindrance and danger of the university and town, as I have often told Mr Mayor and his councillors, the chief whereof is Mr Slegge. I have required Mr Mayor in your honour's name to have special regard to the diligent accomplishing of these things especially at this time. Who giveth fair words, but he doth nothing in deed hitherto. The last composition betwixt the university and the town, made when Sir Thomas Smyth was vice-chancellor, to continue for twenty-one years, was expired five years ago, since which time the mayor and his brethren hath delayed hitherto to agree to any composition for good order and wholesome keeping of the town, wherein the vice-chancellor and the scholars have been always ready.

But the mayor hath promised me within this senyte that he will accomplish the same, the which if he shall not, I shall be compelled to crave your lordship's (*illegible*) and the rest of the honourable company counsell to command the same, or else show some lawful cause to the contrary. For that we are so greatly grieved daily by the annoyance that cometh thereby.

And thus I pray Almighty God long to preserve your L. in most godly and honourable prosperity.

From Cambridge, the eighteenth of this January, 1574.

Your honour's most bounden daily Orator

ANDREW PERNE

(Addressed)

To the *Right Honourable*, the LORD BURGHLEY, *Lord High Treasurer of England, and High Chancellor of the University of Cambridge.*

(Enclosure No. I with DR PERNE's letter of 18 Jan. 1574/5.)

A description of the conveyance of the water from Trumpington Ford unto the King's Ditch, found out by Richard Browne, keeper of the water mills at Lynn, the certainty hereof tried by the level. The thirteenth day of January 1574.

First of all this Richard Browne sayeth that there is in the length from the Nine Wells in Shelford Commons unto the King's Ditch, which is about the space of a mile, six foot fall, so that the water may be brought very well, if so be that the space betwixt the Nine Wells and the Spittle house be brought to be a made ground, for that there being many valleys, these valleys must be made a level ground with earth and clay, that the water may have his free course over it. The other space from the Spittle house unto the King's Ditch is high ground and therefore must have a vault of brick for the water to run through unto the King's Ditch. And thus the water may very well be conveyed this one way.

The charge hereof in brick, mortar, and workmanship, as he sayeth, will come unto the sum of three hundred pounds.

Again the said Browne hath found that the water may be conveyed very well into the King's Ditch another way, that is to say, from the Small Bridges into a pipe of lead six inches high, the length of it four hundred yards. And at the end of this pipe a mill must be made which must force the water to fall into a cistern of lead, and so to run into the said pipe above the level of the ground twenty foot. And thus also the water may very well be brought into the King's Ditch.

The cost and charge of the work this way, for the mill, making the device within the mill, and the pipe of lead, as he maketh his account, will arise to the sum of three hundred pounds. And upon the payment of these sums aforesaid this

Richard Browne hath promised to have himself bound with good and sufficient sureties for the performance hereof.

Memorandum that a thousand and a half of bricks will be sufficient to make thirty foot of the vault that should be from the Spittle house to the King's Ditch which space is thought to be about four hundred yards.

The said Richard Browne sayeth that one foot of the pipe of lead that should go from the cistern of lead at the mill unto the King's Ditch will contain twenty pounds of lead in every foot, and that the space is four hundred yards saving ten wherein the water must be conveyed in a pipe from the said forcing mill unto the King's Ditch. So that the pipe alone will cost six score pounds.

(*Enclosure No.* II with DR PERNE's letter of 18 Jan. 1574/5.)

A declaration of the level of the ground for the conveyance of the water, to be taken from the mills called the King's Mill in Cambridge to the head of the King's Ditch against Pembroke Hall. The which was taken by John Bryant of Cambridge the eighteenth of January 1574.

The said Bryant, taking the measure from the penn of the water of the said mill to the head of the said King's Ditch, doth find the rise to be nine foot, and from the tail and fall of the said water to the said head of the King's Ditch findeth the rise to be sixteen foot. And (*measuring?*) the level of the head of the said King's Ditch to the foot and lowest end of the same, running into the common stream beneath the high bridge against Jesus College Close, he findeth the fall to be twenty foot. So that, from the penn of the water of the said mill to the lowest end of the said King's Ditch, there will be eleven foot fall, and from the water of the lowest tail of the said mill there will be four foot fall.

A great part of the water which cometh to the said King's Mill cometh from Trumpington Ford directly to the said mill, the which mill is distant from the head of the said King's Ditch three score and ten poles after sixteen foot to the pole.

The conveying of this water from the mill to the head of the King's Ditch must be in a gutter or vault made of lime and brick, the which will cost in the whole, as he thinketh, a hundred threescore seventeen pounds and ten shillings. And for this sum he will be bound with good sureties to perform the same.

APPENDIX IV

Copy of *Part* of

An Order of a Court of Sewers,

dated 23 April 1634, preserved in the University
Registry (205, Box B. 19)

The Commissioners who constituted the Court included the Vice-Chancellor and the Mayor. The
Order (1) directs a payment to W. Frost for the
cleansing of the Great River; (2) requires certain
parties to scour out and to repair the New Cut from
Spittle End to Christ's College; and (3) orders certain
improvements of the King's Ditch. Omitting the
first of these three sections, the Order continues:

That Whereas part of the New River and Current is of
late brought from the Spittlehouse End and runneth by and
through part of Emmanuel College and so on to the backside
of the town to Christ's College wall and so down to Walls
Lane End and unto the pound there and so runneth about by
the causey into Jesus College ditch and Nunns Lake, It is
Ordered and Decreed that the said drain shall be from time
to time hereafter cleaned dyked and scoured at the costs and
charges of the Master and Fellows of Christ's and Emmanuel
Colleges as followeth viz: by the said Master and Fellows of
the said colleges from time to time jointly and severally from
and in the places hereafter specified, and that, under such
pains and penalties as in this Order are mentioned, And that

John Entwhistle now brewer of Emmanuel College and his successors shall hereafter keep in good repair the footbridge over the said New Current near Emmanuel Brewhouse by the college wall upon penalty of 20 shillings for every offence, **And that** the Master and Fellows of Christ's College shall hereafter keep in good repair the bridge over the New Drain near to Christ's College wall by their back gate out the street into the Piece by their college orchard wall, upon the like penalty, **And also** shall cleanse the New River current from the pound at Emmanuel Lane End unto Christ's College wall and so into the ditch at Christ's College wall end against Walls Lane, upon penalty of 3/4 for every pole not well and sufficiently cleansed before May 16th yearly, **And that** the Master and Fellows of Emmanuel College through their own grounds shall scour and maintain the banks of the New River, under the same penalty, **And that** the Masters and Fellows of Christ's and Emmanuel Colleges shall jointly maintain that part of the sluice at Spittle End that letteth the water into the said New Current, and all the drains and brick vaults under the ground whereby it passeth to their several colleges and the places particularly assigned to the Master and Fellows of Christ's College, and all the horse and cart bridges over the River, either in the road from Spittle End to Barnwell and from Emmanuel College to Hinton, or unto Jesus Green near the Maids' Causey End, and also the bridge over the River to Ball's Close...yearly by the 16th of May...under penalty of 3/4 per pole and 20 shillings for every bridge not repaired, **Provided always that** the channel of the said New River against Parker's Piece shall be yearly at the said days and times be dyked and scoured by those who have the said Parker's Piece in occupation, **And also that** part of the water of the New River by the consent of the Masters of

Christ's and Emmanuel at such times as they shall think convenient shall be let out by the sluice at Emmanuel End and run down the street and into Christ's College grate into the King's Ditch to cleanse the street in the heat of summer and to increase the water in the King's Ditch in the time of drought and for the benefit of the inhabitants to prevent casualties by fire or other like eminent dangers,

And it is ordered that the King's Ditch and Current of water from Pembroke Hall unto Slaughterhouse Lane shall be made deeper with a small descent to draw the water faster out of Pembroke Hall, and that all stops or stanks that stay or let the current of water in the King's Ditch between Pembroke Hall and Christ's College grate shall be removed before the 16th of May next under penalty of ten shillings for every such stake stank or stopping up.

APPENDIX V

The *Trustees* in 1937 of HOBSON'S CONDUIT TRUST

INDEX

CAMBRIDGE: PRINTED BY WALTER LEWIS, M.A., AT THE UNIVERSITY PRESS